APPLIED SOCIOLINGUISTICS

APPLIED SOCIOLINGUISTICS

An Empirical Study

Dr. Irom Gambhir Singh

AKANSHA PUBLISHING HOUSE
NEW DELHI - 110002 (INDIA)

AKANSHA PUBLISHING HOUSE
4649-B/21,Ansari Road,
Daryaganj, New Delhi-110002
Phones: 23268193, 09435116718
Email: ektabooks@yahoo.com
visit us: www.akanshapublishinghouse.com

Applied Sociolinguistics: An Empirical Study

First Published 2010

ISBN 978-81-8370-213-3

PRINTED IN INDIA

Published by Akansha Publishing House, New Delhi-110002 and printed at Mehra Offset Press, Delhi.

CONTENTS

FOREWORD

In recent years, for a variety of reasons, apart from liberalization and globalization, the question of English, within the broad framework of Applied Sociolinguistics, has grown increasingly complex. Certain issues that seemed so straightforward and so simple not so long ago are now somewhat dramatically different and profoundly complex.

Why and how has all this happened? Has the English problematic changed? Have the paradigms for studying different areas of the role, use and pedagogy of English changed? Clearly the answer to these fundamental questions and many more is a big YES. But then, what precisely is different now? How the sociolinguistics reality of English has changed? Has our methodological approach to the study the Engligh problematic changed? Have fresh theoretical models to study this phenomena have emerged? The present book brilliantly exemplifies this.

John Adams, the second President of the United States had said that English had captured the world. Though many in Europe brushed it aside as megalomania, Adam's prediction has been borne out more thoroughly than even he himself might have imagined. English has pervaded even the most inaccessible. Several factors have been at work. Unprecedented technological advancement and the sweeping economic globalization are perhaps two of the most important developments. The critical issue here is pacing. Everything moves much faster than they did just a decade ago. To boot, culture has intervened in our lives as never before. Very few parts of the world are inaccessible any more. Other people's lives, beliefs, practices, perspectives, and possessions are as familiar to us as our own.

Such enormous spread of English has developed its own self-reinforcing dynamics. This is strikingly noticeable in sociolinguistics. Sociolinguists never tire of declaring that all other languages are just as good and as worthy of study as English. Paradoxically, more sociolinguists live on English than all other languages of the world combined. English has spread and

diversified. Having been indigenized to more societies, communities, and cultures and having adapted to a more wider range of contexts, English has come to encompass local, social and functional variations to such an extent that it uniquely has plural, 'World Englishes.'

Clearly, established sociolinguistics is rooted in Western society in the sense and for similar reasons that imperialism is rooted in the West. English teachers followed the Empire, and so did sociolinguists. One of the most celebrated books about the political background and consequences of the worldwide expansion of English, Robert Phillipson's 1992 *Linguistic Imperialism*, which decries such spread of English as a morally questionable occurrence, is, needless to say, in English.

No doubt, the worldwide diffusion of English holds opportunities and challenges for sociolinguistics. Empirical studies about English, its use and pedagogy, attitudes towards it and motivation for learning it have mostly been on models of social dynamics derived from Western societies. These are, more often than not, unsuitable to explain the predicament of English in the non-Western world from an applied sociolinguistic perspective. The present book is a seminal contribution in that it proposes a non-Western agenda for the study of English phenomenon in all its dimensions, taking into account a variety of extra linguistic factors.

The author explores attitudes to English in the multilingual and pluricultural contexts of Manipur and Assam in particular and all non-native contexts in general. To its credit, it avoids sweeping generalizations based on theoretical orientations and methodologies of Western sociolinguistics. The study emphasizes the need for a more down-to-earth approach; a more concerned and involved engagement with the sociolinguistic reality in totality in non-Western contexts. To that extent this work makes a departure from arm-chair sociolinguistics. Through an empirical study, it explores a number of parameters, dimensions and dynamics of the being and becoming of English. It also indicates significant applications and implications in the area of ELT/ESL. To boot, it uniquely signifies history as society and society as history. The study certainly opens many corners for explorations of English from an applied sociolinguistics perspective.

—Kailash S. Aggarwal

ACKNOWLEDGEMENTS

I am grateful to my supervisor, Dr. Kailash S. Aggarwal, for introducing me to this area of research in sociolinguistics and for his whole-hearted initiative and guidance in shaping my professional career; without him it would have been difficult to have completed such an important task.

I owe my sincere gratitude to all my teachers, friends and well-wishers for their encouragement in the completion of my work. I specially extend my heartiest thanks to the respondents from Assam and Manipur for their unfailing support to fill up the questionnaires and interacting with me over extended periods of time.

I shall ever remain thankful to Shri Diganta Gohain, Department of Assamese, Chaiduar College, Gohpur, Assam, for his translation of the questionnaire into Assamese and other valuable suggestions during the fieldwork.

I am also thankful to Dr. R.K. Ranjan, Director, Academic Staff College, Manipur University, Canchipur and Dr. Gurudas Das, Head, Department of Humanities, National Institute of Technology, Silchar, Assam for their moral and physical support in getting this work published.

—Irom Gambhir Singh

INTRODUCTION

Theoretical and applied sociolinguistics has developed in recent times as a challenging field of study. The development of this discipline may be traced partly to a reaction against formal models and methods, and partly to a greater pressure from various competing and conflicting speech communities as well as to the demands made by policy decision-makers. In our broad understanding, applied sociolinguistics deals with the social, economic and political implications of basic inequalities in language competence and use in a variety of domains of public life. This is perhaps of much greater significance when we deal with a transplanted language such as English in the post-colonial societies of Asia and Africa.

Controversies about the enslaving and liberating role that English can and does play by its continuous use in independent societies and nations have by now become redundant and of much less use to policy decision-makers as well as the common masses of people. What has gripped scholars in recent times is the question related to the power and Politics of English in these societies Noam Chomsky, the icon of contemporary linguistics has been reported to have stated that questions of language really and basically relate to questions of power; but, then, he goes on to assert that such questions were beyond the scope of linguistics proper. While conceding Chomsky's point as a matter of opinion we are ceased with the disturbing point of narrowing down linguistic studies to the study of 'grammar.' Such a limited point of view regarding linguistics closes the doors on investigations into interesting areas such as linguistic power and politics, which subsume questions of language inequalities, language discrimination and linguistic human rights.

The proposition to view a linguistic system as an autonomous entity and a self-contained whole is asocial and apolitical.

Historically, most of the standard languages of Europe established national linguistic sovereignty after undergoing intense political struggle and nationalistic assertion. These processes determined, to a large extend, the European intellectual tradition and a fundamentally monolingual perspective for a long period. A corollary to this was a widely accepted assumption that the countries of Europe were linguistically homogeneous in some sense in which there was a direct correlation between the names of countries, peoples and languages.

In most sociolinguistic setting in the third world, however, such a direct or even indirect association between countries, people and languages is virtually non-existent. As a matter of fact, a number of names applied, and apply even today, to what the colonial masters refered to by one name. For example, 'Manipuri' or 'Meeteilon; 'Manipur', 'Kangleipak' or 'Meeteileipak' are different names that apply to the same linguistic and geopolitical entity. It is the European monolingual perspective which guided the British colonial officers and investigators to present entirely confused and confusing accounts of the language scenario in British India.

The nature and extent of linguistic heterogeneity in India has been trumpeted out of proportion by academicians, statemen and media personnel, apart from others. No doubt, forces of ethnolinguistic identity, more often than not associated with social, economic and political forces, have created pressures towards assertions of divergent micro-level identities. At the same time, pressures towards linguistic and associated assimilation or homogeneity have been created by processes and institutions such as literacy programmes, language standardisation, centralised administrative structures, schooling and the mass media etc., particularly during the half-a-century of India's Independence. The later factors have contributed to the lingua-francas and metropolitan languages such as English and Hindi as well as Bengali, Marathi and Tamil at the national and regional levels. By common sense, these factors could have and should have led to lesser linguistic and greater language convergence. It did happen in the United States of America, in North America particularly, where the 'melting pot' led to substantial erosion

of many aspects of ethnic and linguistic identity, till as recent as the 1960s and 1970s. In the case of India, it is far too complex since both the processes of language convergence and divergence have paralleled to each other, without any clear indication of the shape that the linguistic scenario is heading towards.

A number of recent studies in the West as well as in India have attempted to link intra-and inter-linguistic variation in a speech community with stratificational variables like race, ethnicity, caste, clan and class etc. It is beyond any shred of doubt that these studies have made substantial contribution to our understanding of the language phenomena but, a major drawback of these approaches issues out of fact that they take for granted an assumption that individual speakers could be grouped into neat social classes and categories. Quite often, variation within the speech community is either not taken cognisance of or ignored. Unfortunately we have been trapped in a vicious circle of highlighting the individual speaker and the nation-state, with no meaningful advances made to match our studies with the ground realities as they obtain from time to time.

Another interesting area of sociolinguistic research has been to examine minority and marginalised languages and to look at linguistic inequalities in terms of social status, economic opportunities and political power. Since a community's control over a language is quite often directly related to educational, employment, economic, political and related opportunities, this is an area which demands greater attention and which ironically has received the least attention. For example, the medium of instruction has often been cited as the main cause of school failure. The school, being the society's most powerful shaping instrument, exerts great control over its future, most of the schools engender the powerful and marketable values of language and knowledge which in the present Indian context happen to be the English language and Western knowledge. Children who come from non English, non Western backgrounds experience physical, psychological and emotional conflict throughout their schooling. In fact, sociolinguists have argued that, such educational, psychological and socio-cultural conflict and failure lead the children to various forms of crime and anti-social activities,

alcoholism and drug addiction and such other negative consequences.

Given this broad understanding of the role of language in determining an individual's, a society's and a nation's future, it becomes urgently imperative to study the various aspects of the power and politics of English, or to that extend any legitimised language, in its various dimensions and implications. English assumes the greatest importance since it has come to exert virtually monopolistic dominance over all instrumental domains. The dominance of English in all spheres has increased manyfold since the 1990's, particularly after India's adoption of the liberalization and globalization policies. Hence, we approach the issue with a broad understanding that English is increasingly becoming a precondition for civic existence. We, of course, do realise that the language has no and cannot have any existence apart from the totality of its users. English has not existed on its own nor does it simply reflect any pre-existent reality.

Various theoretical as well as methodological models approaches and frameworks are available for the study of the English problematic in India. We have discussed some of the major ones in Chapter-1. However, we would like to argue that they lack in operational value and have not been of much help to us for situating and explaining the findings of our study which have been discussed in Chapter-2 (Secondary information) and Chapter-4 (empirical study). We have no hesitation in proposing that they have been found to be untenable to a large extent in the light of the historical, social, political and linguistic developments in the North-East in recent decades as well as by the findings of our empirical study, though limited a number of ways.

There are a number of strong methods for analysing evidence on the power and politics of English. Again, unfortunately, they lack in adequate explanatory power. But, most significantly, during our exploration we found them of very little use in presenting, analysing and understanding our own data. Therefore, we had no choice but to adopt a simple arithmetic approach to our data but, combining with it our own intuitive and critical observations and insights.

On the whole, we have made a preliminary attempt in the study to approach the question of 'power' and 'politics' of 'English' from a multidimensional and empirical perspective. As pointed out earlier, we have not depended on any theoretical or methodological model or framework; rather, we have gone with the study and approached it commonsensically, as the reality unfolded before us. We have gathered a good amount of socio-historical, political, cultural and related information on the two focal communities (ethnic Assamese and ethnic Meeteis) from secondary sources. Hence, Chapter-2 may appear as bigger than it could be, but in our understanding it forms a very significant backgrounder to the not-so-adequate empirical data. We assume that we have made some advances and developed some useful insights into the problematic, inspite of our many limitations that we have honestly reported throughout this study.

Let us now present an abstraction of the present work that follows. An attempt has been made in the present study to develop a socio-pedagogic perspective on the power and politics of English in north-east India. From the researcher's point of view, this work assumes its relevance and significance for primarily three reasons. Firstly, it is the first work of its kind not only relating to north-east India, but the entire country as well. No doubt, a number of research work into the power and politics of English has been done in a few universities, but none of these have been comparative and as comprehensive as the present one. Most of them have delimited their studies to very few aspects, emphasizing the linguistic aspect at the expense of socio-historical and related aspects. Therefore, the present study heavily focuses the sociolinguistic and sociological dimensions. Secondly, the present work attempts to combine theoretical perspective and empirical data in a meaningful way. And, thirdly, even though the study is located in north-east India, with specific focus on the Brahmaputra Valley and the Manipur Valley, its findings have much wider implications, specificities of the two valleys notwithstanding. On the whole, while concentrating on the trees, the study does not lose sight of the forest.

Chapter 1, entitled "The Power and Politics of English: A Theoretical Exploration", deals with the theoretical notions and

concepts related to the two basic terms of "power" and "politics". We first critically examine these two terms in general and then go on to relate them to power. As the term "power" is used in relation to language, we get a metaphor to charactesise language as the "loaded weapon", to use Dwight Bolinger's phrase. Starting from the fundamental question, viz. "What is linguistic power?", the study goes on to examine different approaches to language and power, with reference to the five major models (correlative, domain, conflict, functional and verbal repertoire) used in the literature. While not undermining the usefulness of these models, we find them problematic to due serious terminological and methodological confusion.

In the following section, the study deals with Foucault's approach to power and emphasises the need to address fundamental questions relating to the destination, possession, operation, network and ideological production of power. These questions keep on recurring as we go on to examine the global spread of English and motivations for such spread that results in the acquisition of power. In the next two sections of the first Chapter, we deal with the question of the strategies of language power and politics and the strategies used for gaining "range" and "depth" for English language at the international level. The following sections examine English's spheres of power and control, its role in the devalorisation of a host of indigenous languages in the Outer Circle and the concomitant politics in the Inner Circle. Lastly, by relating Foucault's approach to linguistic power, the Chapter concludes by dealing with the ideological implications with regard to English. The Chapter suggests that, in addition to examining, carefully and critically, theoretical, albeit speculative, questions on the interplay of the language "power" and language "politics", local empirical questions need to be asked pointedly.

Chapter 2, namely "Locating the study: the North-East Scenario: a Review of Sociolinguistic and ELT Contexts," first provides a brief description of the north-east problematic, emphasising the distinctiveness and individuality of the Brahmaputra Valley and the Manipur Valley. Next, we have provided a socio-historical account of the origin and development of the two ethnolinguistic communities, viz. Assamese and Meeteis,

as a backgrounder to the study. The course of Sanskritisation, de-Sanskritisation and the consequent search for the roots, has been outlined in adequate detail. The paramount importance of ethno-linguistic identity among the two communities have been highlighted. While not undermining the internal disparity within each community, we have taken two groups as significant categories in order to resource their ethnolinguistic, social, cultural, political, economic and educational manifestations and expressions. Such ethnolinguistic categorisation does not meaningfully reflect the dynamics of power and politics of English in its being and becoming. Lastly, in the Chapter, we provide detailed accounts of the beginnings, development and the present context of English education in the two valleys. It has been emphasised that, quite unlike mainstream India, no anti-English feelings or sentiments exist (or existed) among the populations in the two valleys. Rather, not quite surprising though, anti-Indian language (anti-Bengali in the case of ethnic Assamese and anti-Hindi in the case of Meeteis) feelings have surfaced during prolonged movements aimed at historical correction and valorisation of regional languages. This Chapter is of prime importance as, on the one hand it provides historical, sociological, ethnic, economic, political and related information, as a realistic backgrounder, for locating and appreciating the empirical study; it outlines the pre-colonial and post-colonial ELT contexts on the other.

Chapter 3, titled "The Empirical Study", is a brief one that describes the objectives and methodology of the empirical study. The objectives are to seek answers, rather, to be able to articulate meaningful questions, questions that do not apparently and directly relate to the power and politics of English, but have important implications for them. The heart of the matter is that issues relating to power and politics in general, and to the language (English) in particular, are mostly tricky and remain covert. Thus, the only way out is to examine these issues covertly, though the exploration of a variety of linguistic and extralinguistic dimensions. The methodology employed in the study is the traditional questionnaire survey, and the sampling is more intuitive and selective. What makes the empirical study interesting in a

novel way is that it relates and juxtaposes the researcher's diary notes, involved and concerned observations and institutions as a "participant" in both of the communities concerned.

Chapter 4, "The Field Survey", presents the results of the field survey conducted during 1989-99 among respondents belonging to different genders, age groups, income groups, educational attainment and professional/occupations. The respondents belong to a cross-section of people such as 'professionals' (doctors, engineers, lawyers etc); media persons (reporters and journalists); security personnel (police, paramilitary and army personnel); general administrators (civil official of high rank); educational administrators (principals, directors of education, University officers etc); private and public sector employees; performing and creative artists; NGO activists, politicians, sports personalities and house wives etc, and most importantly, teachers and students.

Contrasting descriptive statistics with inferential statistics, the responses to more than hundred question items have been presented in tabular form, in terms of absolute figures as well as percentages. Meaningful inferences have been made from these tables. The results of the field study covering the respondents' sociolinguistic background, linguistic competence, medium of self-education, relative proficiency in the mother tongue and in English, use of English in different domains, mode and tenor of discourse and in the media have been presented in this Chapter, in total figures as well as comparative (between Assam and Manipur) figures. To uncover the covert impact of the power and politics of English and the individual respondents' subjective response to and perception of this impact has been unveiled through a series of jumbled questions that bring out their attitudes, loyalty and subjectivity. This Chapter demonstrates the vast complexity of the topic under research, particularly in the places where the results do not neatly match well-formulated theories.

In the last Chapter 5, "Findings and Conclusions", we have attempted to correlate competence in use of and attitudes towards English, which do not correlate in fact. The pedagogic applications and implications of the present study, focusing

English education in north-east India, have been grappled with. We have unambiguously conceded that a number of vital questions remain unanswered, but, then, we have also suggested the lines along which further research could be conducted. The exhaustive "Bibliography" at the end should be of use to researchers who would venture into this field in future. We have argued all through that there is a great need for more and more empirical investigations adopting a multidisciplinary perspective and without any theoretical bias. The present study has been presented as a humble attempt toward that end.

1

THE POWER AND POLITICS OF ENGLISH: A THEORETICAL EXPLORATION

When the term "power" used in relation to 'language', we get a metaphor to characterise language as the "loaded weapon", to use Bolinger's phrase (Bolinger 1980). The targets of the weapon, its range of ammunitions and individual and social consequences of the use of this weapon have yet to be studied seriously. No doubt in the past, the power of the language of religion (e.g. Sanskrit in India), had attracted considerable attention. More recently the use of language in domains of law, medicine, media and so on has developed as a special field of study. The study of language and politics, both general and specific, including micro-level case studies, however, is different. We shall examine it a little later.

In the present study, we have a modest aim i.e. to present some empirical evidence on randomly selected issues related to the power and politics of the global spread of English, restricting the study to the states of Manipur and Assam in India. There does not exist, or I am not aware of, any theoretical framework for such a study. But, I hope, this study, while briefly addressing the specific theoretical issues concerning English, shall focus on empirical evidence. Such evidence would hopefully contribute to our understanding of some aspects of the complexity of describing the relationship between language and power.

Let us begin with a word of caution: questions about language and power need not be necessarily or exclusively linguistic issues. Often, the issues go beyond linguistics into the realms

of history, sociology, pedagogy, psychology (i.e. attitude and motivation), political and economic considerations. Thus the topic of our study has many faces, and the power of English has yet to be studied from all of these perspectives. This study, needless to stress, reveals only a minute tip of the iceberg.

The two crucial terms of this study, the "power" and "politics" of English, are linked in more than one way; the first implies the attainment of various types of "control" and the second signifies the processes and strategies used for this control (see, e.g. Kramarae et al. 1985). Once a language attains power, it does not mean that political strategies are necessarily abandoned-far from it. Rather, it is a vicious circle: in order for power and control to be maintained, political manoeuvering must continue which, then, develops into various situations of conflict (for discussions of case studies of language conflict, see, e.g. Aggarwal 1991; Annamalai 1979; Bourhis 1984; Brass 1974; Das Gupta 1970; among others).

The fundamental question that confronts us here is: How do power and politics relate to language? The power of language is intimately, though in quite complex and insidious ways, linked with societal power of various types. The dimensions of power and resultant politics include:

a) the spread of a language to numerically expand the speech community (Cooper 1982);

b) the use of a language as a vehicle of cultural, religious and other types of "enlightenment" (this applies to English in several ways - we will return to this question a little later) ; and

c) the use of a language with one or more of the following motives:

- to deculturize people from their own indigenous traditions (e.g. the use of Persian in parts of Northern India; the use of Sanskrit in Manipur from 18th century onwards);
- to gain economic advantage;
- to control various domains of knowledge and information, particularly in the fields of governance, science and technology;

- to use the language for deception ('colonisation of mind', cultural hegemony); and
- to create a circle of dependency on a country, nation, culture, technology and so forth.

The concerns for power, and its reflection in various types of politics, show up in different ways at different times. For example, almost half-a-century ago, when George Orwell addressed the issue of the politics of the English language, his concern was to provide a "catalogue of swindles and perversions" (Orwell 1986: 162) which had entered the English language - especially in the political writing. Orwell was not the first to address the "decay" of the English language; Cassandras predicting the doom of English are still alive and active (cf. Greenbaum 1985). The concern of this study however, is very different from that of Orwell: it is not to say that the "present political chaos is connected with the decay of language" (Orwell 1968: 169).

The two key terms, "power" and "politics", are used here in the context of their interplay within the three concentric circles of English: the 'Inner Circle', 'The Outer Circle', and the 'Expanding Circle' (cf. Kachru 1985). As Kachru has explained in quite elegant terms, (we shall discuss them later), these three Circles represent three distinct types of speech fellowships of English, phases of the spread of the language, and particular characteristics of the uses of the language and its learning/ acquisition and linguistic innovations/abberrations. There is, of course, an interplay of politics - and conflict - within each Circle. This aspect of English merits a detailed study in its own right, as does the study of the politics, which the countries in the Inner Circle are playing against the Outer Circle.

WHAT IS LINGUISTIC POWER?

The study of linguistic power is not identical to the study of state power, conceding that there might be some similarities and further conceding that linguistic power is ultimately related to state power. Linguistic power has to be understood essentially through symbols and manipulation of the symbols. Linguistic power may manifest itself in the modification of Linguistic behavior in one or more of the following ways: first, by adding a code to the linguistic repertoire of a speech community or a

speech fellowship. This may be done by the use of one or more of the following power strategies: (a) persuasion; (b) regulation; (c)inducement; and/or (d)force. Second, the same goals may be achieved by the suppression of a particular variety and the elevation of another variety. The arms or means of suppression need not be always direct or obvious (see, e.g. Wolfson and Manes 1985).

All of the above strategies have been used in the case of the spread of English in South Asia, South East Asia and African countries as elsewhere. However, in order to study this phenomenon, one has to start, as it were from the beginning: look for a conceptual framework, so that some generalization could be attempted. Below, we will attempt to provide such an overview.

APPROACHES TO LANGUAGE AND POWER

The concepts of "power" and "politics" have been extensively discussed in various disciplines. However, so far, the discussion of the relationship between these two concepts and language in general and English in particular, has been based on very few empirical case studies, some anecdotal statement in the literature and some quantitative attitude studies. No doubt, sociolinguistics and sociology of language do provide several frameworks to establish a relationship between language and society. While some of them focus on linguistic data, others have other orientations: political, sociological, economic and so on. Let us briefly mention six models here.

1. The Correlative Model

This model establishes covariation between the formal linguistic features and sociological contexts of various types (e.g. caste, class, status, sex etc (see, e.g. Dittmar; Labov 1970). This model is not necessarily meant to establish a language and power relationship. However such studies as of caste, class, economic status etc. do provide good indicators for power related interpretations.

2. The Domain Model

This model studies the use of a language or speech variety with reference to preferred domain allocations. It has been used

both in monolingual (as in style and register shift) and multilingual societies (as in language shift). For further discussion on this model, see, e.g. Fishman 1971, 1989 among others.

3. The Conflict Model

This model as Nicholas (1985: 36) observes, emphasizes "the economic basis of class divisions and sees them as organized in relation to the mode of production: it stresses exploitation, oppression and social conflict as important factors in social organization." The terms "exploitation" and "oppression" are vital here. Within this approach, language may be seen as an instrument of exploitation and oppression and this perception may result in conflict. It is important to note that both of these terms have been used with reference to English and it varieties.

4. The Functional Model

The functional model has been associated with several schools of linguistics. One major characteristic of these schools is that language is seen essentially as an instrument of social interaction (see, e.g. the work of the British linguist J.R.Firth, discussed in Kachru 1981; Halliday 1978; Dittmar 1976 and Pride 1979). The "interactionist model" used by sociolinguists may also be accommodated under this approach. According to this view, social organization places relations between people at the center and recognizes that human interaction is a shaping process in its own right"(Nichols 1984).

5. The Verbal Repertoire Model

The verbal repertoire concept recognizes the linguistic and functional co-existence of languages, language varieties, and styles within the repertoire of one person or of a speech community. The choices of codes depend on the perceived power of a code in terms of functions, participants, situations and so on. In the verbal repertoire model, the power of a code is seen as much in establishing an identity by the use of a particular code as in suppressing it by the use of another code. One sees this phenomenon, for example, in using English for the neutralization of identities in several multilingual societies. In recent studies on "code alteration"(code-mixing and code-switching), several cross-cultural generalizations have been made about the perceived power of English (Kachru 1982).

Now, what is the relevance of these approaches to the study of language and power? There are several ways in which these approaches can be useful to our understanding of the relationship between the two: first, to provide validation for extralinguistic indicators of power or non power in terms of the distribution of language features as has been shown in studies on caste and class (ibid); second, to study the power basis for attitudes to and preferences for a language, its varieties, styles and registers; third, to understand the question of language and identity; fourth, to see if language change, especially in language contact situations, has a relationship with the perception of power, domination and/or imposition of a language, and fifth, to study the phenomenon of language modernization and its relationship to a particular language (see, e.g., Krishnamurti and Mukherjee 1984 for the impact of English on news media in India).

There are other approaches and other uses of the approaches too. Further, these approaches are not mutually exclusive: the difference is in the underlying assumptions and the focus of each approach. Some of these models are primarily language-centered (e.g. the correlative model and functional model), and some are extra-language centered: (e.g. the conflict model). But, none of these approaches has been used to interpret linguistic power per se, nor is it the primary goal of these models to do so. However, several "socially-realistic" linguistic studies do provide vital insights into the understanding of linguistic power in terms of language use as, for example in the approaches of J.R. Firth, Michael Halliday, William Labov, and Dell Hymes, to name just four.

The problem is not just that linguists have generally ignored these aspects of language study; there is also serious terminological confusion since each discipline interprets power differently, and offers different methodologies for analysis and interpretation of power.

FOUCAULT'S APPROACH TO POWER

It is worthwhile to note that in linguistic there still is very little grasp of power related issues, for these issues have not been the main concern of the major paradigms of linguistics, or,

for that matter, even of sociolinguistics. Here one finds it useful to go beyond the traditional boundaries of linguistics and sociolinguistic and explore approaches of scholars in other areas/ disciplines.

In doing so, we immediately think of the insightful discussion by Michael Foucault (1972-77) on different topics related to power. However, even Foucault confirms that "... power and its strategies, at once general and detailed and its mechanisms have never been studied." (Foucault 1980). What do we mean by strategies of power? Let's go back to Foucault to seek some illumination. In his view, "strategies in the exploitation of possibilities which it[power] itself discerns and creates" (ibid). Here, there are two assertions of power: (i) that power is exercised and exists in action; and (ii) that power is a relation of force. In that sense, power becomes an organ of repression. In Foucault's vision, the schemata for the analysis of power are: contact-oppression schema and domination oppression schema. Before we proceed further in exploring Foucault's assertions about power, it is necessary to answer questions closer to language concerns.

1. Is Foucault's basic assertion applicable to the understanding of language?
2. Is linguistic power always an instrument of oppression?
3. How does linguistic power manifest itself in a speech community?

The answer to the first two questions varies from case to case. The manifestations of linguistic power have a wide range: from crude, physical linguistic power through pragmatic power to the subtle, indirect psychological pressures. An example of crude linguistic power is the imposition of Japanese on the Koreans and the Malays during World War II, or, if we go a little back, the imposition of Bengali script and Sanskrit vocabulary in Manipur in the eighteenth century. Indirect psychological pressure, on the other hand, is evident when languages make claims of "other world" power. This power is attributed to a language in the context of the religion, e.g. the recitation of Sanskrit hymns; the power of japa (chanting), the "reward" for the reading of The *Q'uaran*, and so forth. This power of language

is unique since it must be accepted without questions; one accepts it as an inherent power of language. Somewhere in the middle of the two extremes lies pragmatic power of language which all of us experience in our daily lives. In fact, one aim of language education is to teach us the pragmatic successes and failures of various languages, varieties of languages and styles. At present, English has the greatest pragmatic success in a wide variety of domains across cultures. Though this proposition could be debated over, we shall deal with it later.

Going back to Foucault, let us try to summarize his suggestions for what he terms "methodological precautions" (1980) for the study of power. One has to ask, as Foucault suggests, questions such as the following:

1. What is the ultimate "destination of power" at its "extremities"?
2. What is the aim of someone who possesses power? In other words, who has the power and what does the person have in mind?
3. What is the network of power? In Foucault's view, power "must be analysed as something which circulates, or rather as something which only functions in the form of a chain" (1980: 98).
4. What are the agents of power?
5. What are the "ideological productions" of power?

In the sections that follow, we will address some of the questions raised by Foucault, with the specific reference to English.

Language Spread and Motivations for the Acquisition of Power

Motivations for the acquisition of various types of power has been particularly strong for the languages associated with colonial expansion: English, Portuguese, Spanish, to name few major languages.

Turning to English, during its expansion on various continents, its speakers have claimed and sought different types of power for it. The language has also been perceived by other to symbolize such power. Consider, for example, the following:

1. Enlightenment in a religious sense

The term "enlightenment" is used here in the context of religious indoctrination, proselytization, and otherworldly reward. Note the following observation concerning India:

The true curse of darkness is the introduction of light. The Hindus err, because they are ignorant and their errors have never fairly been laid before them. The communication of our light and knowledge to them would prove the best remedy for their disorders. (Grant 1831-32:60-61)

In Sri Lanka, the situation was not very different. There, a "Christian institution was set up in 1827 to give a superior education to a number of young persons who from their ability, piety, and good conduct were likely to prove fit persons in communicating a knowledge of Christianity to their countrymen." (Barnes 1932: 43).

The American approach to the Philippines was identical to the British approach to South Asia. In the U.S. President Mckinley's view,

> there was nothing else for us to do but to take them all, and to educate the Filipinos, and uplift and civilize and christianize them, and by God's grace do the very best we could for them, as our fellowmen for whom Christ also died (cited in Mazrui 1975: 201).

It was one way of conscience-soothing, using power with the motive of the otherworldly reward. This resulted in developing "the power elite" of a type previously unknown to the regions of Asia and Africa. Mazrui rightly asserts that "Christianity in Africa .... is the religion of the power in the majority of countries south of Sahara" (Mazrui 1975: 11-12).

2. Marker of the "civilizing process"

Broadly speaking, one might refer to the "civilizing process" as the development of material and intellectual potential through various processes of modernisation /westernisation. The western literature is full of examples of this attitude on the part of many westerners in Asia and Africa. Smith's (1986) dissertation on "Papua New Guinea English" includes two very interesting quotations from important scholars teaching English in Papua

New Guinea. One scholar took the position that "English per se is the most valuable gift we can bestow on the native" (cited in Smith 1986: 11), and the other, who later became the first Vice-chancellor of the University of Papua New Guinea , said in 1958, "... teach them English, and more English: this is what they want" (*ibid*: 14).

3. Distancing from native cultures

This is interrelated with the motivation of the "civilizing process". An extreme example of this çlaim is the often-quoted observation of T.B. Macaulay (1800-1859):

> I have no knowledge of either Sanskrit or Arabic. But I have done what I could to form a correct estimate of their value ... I am quite ready to take the Oriental learning at the valuation of the Orientalists themselves. I have never found one amongst them who could deny that a single shelf of a good European library was worth the whole native literature of India and Africa [Sharp 1920-1922].

The United States, as Zentella observes (1981: 219), tried to Americanize Puerto Rico "with a vengeance during the fifty years of its occupation." The aim was, as the then Commissioner of Education, Victor Clark saw it, quite clear:

> If the schools became Americans and the teachers and the students were guided by the American spirit, then the island would be essentially American in sympathies, opinions, and attitudes towards government.

This attitude change would result in an immense social change and the ultimate result would be similar to what we have seen in Africa and South Asia, the creation of "Afro-Saxons"(Mazrui 1975: 11) and "Brown Sahibs".

4. Acquisition of various spheres of knowledge

English has by now become a major tool for acquiring knowledge in the sciences, technology, and even the humanities and social sciences. Its "vehicular load", to use the term suggested by Quirk et. at. (1972:2), is indeed unprecedented for a human language: "Vehicular load" refers to the extent to which a language is ".... a medium of science or literature or other highly regarded cultural manifestations including the way of life" (ibid: 2)Indeed, English does not represent only "the way of life" of the Inner

Circle but that of countries within the Outer Circle too. And there lies its strength as an international language.

5. Vehicle of pragmatic success

The pragmatic success of English is not restricted to international context only. Its success is evident in the Outer Circle for international roles. This aspect has been widely discussed in the literature and the terms "link," "contact," and "complementary" languages are used to refer to this function of English (see, e.g. Agnihotri & Khanna 1992).

STRATEGIES FOR POWER AND POLITICS "RANGE" AND "DEPTH"

In the global context, the two important indicators of the power of English are its "range" and "depth." "Range" refers to the total domains of function and the types of the functions which the language has acquired around the world. At present, English dominates the larger spectrum of the functions in widest possible register range. With the digital revolution and the Internet, this domination of English over the functional domains is increasing very fast, notwithstanding the outcry against language imperialism and other such anti-English slogans.

Let us look at some parameters of the power of English which attest to the present and expanding range and depth of the language.

Parameters of the Power of English

a. *Demographic and numerical*: There is unprecedented spread across cultures and languages, on practically every continent (see, e.g. Fishman *et al.* 1977; Crystal 1985).

b. *Functional*: English provides access to most important scientific, technological, and cross - cultural domains of knowledge and interaction.

c. *Attitudinal*: English symbolizes one or more of the following: neutrality, liberalism, status, and progressivism

d. *Accessibility*: English provides international accessibility in the Outer Circle and international mobility across regions (cf. "link language", "complimentary language", "contest language" and so an and so forth).

e. *Pluricentricity*: The recent loosening of the 'centre' of English has resulted in the nativization and acculturation of the language. These two are, then, responsible for the "assimilation" of English across cultures.

f. *Material*: English is the most efficient tool for mobility, economic gains and social status.

The term "depth" here is viewed in a horizontal sense - the societal penetration of English - In educated and other varieties. However, the demography of Language "penetration" - in a societal sense - is only marginally important. It is the social and educational levels of the users of English, which seem to carry more weight.

One just has to ask questions of the following types to understand the power of English across cultures:

1. What is one's reaction towards a complete and proficient user of a language in the Outer or Expanding Circles?
2. Are the roles acquired by English users emulative?
3. What are the economic motivations for learning English?
4. What are the uses of English in terms of intranational and international mobility?

Now, is there any way to mark the indicators of the depth of English - linguistic and societal? The depth of the language in terms of social penetration is rather difficult to assess. However, there are two indicators for it. First, with regard to the pluricentricity of English and the "shifting" of the centre of English, the following observation of Steiner (1975: 4) is very apt:

> The first most oblivious point to make is that the linguistic centre of English has shifted. This is so demographically, Great Britain now makes up only a small portion of the English speaking totality. 'Totality', furthermore, is quiet a wrong word. The actual situation is only of nearly incommensurable variety and flux. Any map of "world English" today even without being either exhaustive or minutely detailed, would have to include the forms of the language as spoken in many areas of east, west and South Africa, in India, Ceylon and United States, possessions or spheres of presence in the Pacific. It would have to list Canadian English, the speech of Australia, that of New Zealand and above

> all, of course, the manifold shades of America parlance. Yet, although such a catalogue would compromise hundreds of millions of English-speakers whose idiolects and communal usage would vary all the way from West Indian speech to New South Wales and the Yukan, it would be very far from complete.

And, Steiner, in his typical tone, goes much further and asserts:

> But this shift of the linguistic centre involves a more than statistics. It does look as if the principal energies of the English language, as if its genius for acquisition for innovation, for metaphoric response, had also moved away from England... (1975: 5).

Pluricentricity has further led to pluralism in incorporating other cultural and literary traditions: African, South East Asian, South Asian, and so on. And, the result is that English is no more an exponent of only the Judeo-Christian traditions and western concepts of literary creativity (see, e.g. Kachru 1983). The varieties within an institutionalized variety in the Outer Circle have provided "access" to various strata of society. Such varieties may be mutually exclusive, or not – so – exclusive, or may involve a lectal shift, as for example, in the case of the basilect in Singapore, Nigerian Pidgin in Nigeria and Bazaar English in India.

Though the demography of English cannot be underestimated, it should be mentioned that the "range" of functions is a better indicator of the power of English than is its depth. In fact, on account of "range", one can accuse English of causing functional "dormancy" in a number of major and minor languages of the world. The "maintenance" of "other" language (i.e. a vast number of mother tongues) under the overwhelming power of English must be seen within this perspective. This association is often presented as an argument against the use of English. One, therefore, sees that the policies of a government, - or, the recognition of an indigenous language for a particular role as in most states of India – does not seem to be effective under the "power" of English. While emotional attachment may be to one's own language, pragmatic needs motivate not only the continued use of English, but also its further expansion. It is indeed a linguistic vicious circle.

STRATEGIES OF GAINING RANGE AND DEPTH

One might pause here to ask: How did English acquire its unprecedented range and depth? A number of answers have been given in the literature. No doubt, the major reason is the historical role of England as a colonial power, with English being the linguistic tool of that political might. Other strategies, not always consciously planned, come to mind.

(a) The 'camel-in-the-tent' strategy

This strategy was typically applied in parts of Africa and South Asia. In these regions, English first gained a highly restricted foothold and later, with political manoeuvering and other tactics, expanded the range. In some cases, the role of missionaries, though not always conscious or planned, had been substantial. This is most apparent in the case of East Africa. In South Asia, the role of missionaries varied from one part of the region to another.

(b) The 'linguistic elitism' strategy

The political power naturally attributed a "power" to the language of the British Raj.

(c) The 'close the ranks' strategy

This was essentially a language solidarity strategy. Those who wanted identity with the political power first had to establish an identity of a shared code.

(d) The 'information control' strategy

The power of English is not exclusively due to information "control" in the domains of science and technology. In the Outer Circle, for example, information control had other manifestations, too. English was, and continues to be – the language of the legal system, the language of higher education, the language a pan-regional and / or pan-Indian administrative network, and so on (see, e.g. Bailey and Gorlach 1982; Kachru 1985).

(e) *The 'marketability' strategy*

English is already a major language of trade, commerce, banking, and international advertising. In the Outer Circle, English additionally performs several localized roles either because the

indigenous languages are not equipped for these roles – as they have not been used in such contexts before – or because the use of English is considered prestigious or "powerful". This attitude has bestowed more power upon the language. We will not dwell on this point in great detail because this topic has been discussed sufficiently in the literature (see, e.g. Aggarwal 1984; Verma 1995; Agnihotri and Khanna 1992; Kachru 1984 among others).

THE SPHERE OF POWER AND CONTROL

What are the current domains and spheres of control which provide evidence of an interplay of power and politics related to the English language? And, what are the pressure groups, which control the strings of power? The answer to the first question is perhaps easier than it is to the second question. There are four basic areas in which the power of English manifests itself: linguistic, literary, attitudinal, and pedagogical. The manifestation of this power has been described, and, of course, attacked, under different provocative labels: discrimination (Leibonitz 1969); imperialism (Haugen 1985); genocide (Day 1985); inequality (Sato 1985) and death, to list only a few such terms.

First, let us consider the question of linguistic control. This reflects in the following ways, among others:

(a) the use of channels of codification and the control of these channels;

(b) the attitude towards linguistic innovation by those who are not part of the Inner Circle. This is however, not restricted to the Outer Circle; there are "linguistic lames" in the Inner Circle, too, as has been shown in several studies, notably by Willian Labov;

(c) lexicographical research and the choice of dictionary – worthy entries.

These three channels of linguistic control are most powerful since they can define, as we know, it is only the powerful who can define others and make their definition stick. And, by having their definitions accepted, they appropriate more power.

The second aspect to consider is the ethnocentric attitude toward literary creativity in English in the Outer Circle (see, e.g.

Dissanayake 1985). This altitude is expressed in subtle ways by establishments in the departments of English language and literature, in professional journals, and in professional organizations. There is already an impressive body of data available on this point. The result of such control is that the authentication of non – native writers in English primarily depends on the Inner Circle.

The third aspect is attitudinal. Here, we get involved in complex psychological and sociological issues concerning the identities of individuals, of speech communities, and of speech fellowships. One would like to believe that issues of attitude apply only to the Outer Circle; actually; this is not the case. We now have an abundance of literature to show that the power and politics of some selected groups have equal sway in the Inner Circle on some "disadvantaged" segments of society (see, e.g. Nichols 1985).

The fourth aspect is concerned with the "pedagogic issues" in the teaching of English in the international contexts. In other words, it refers to the power, a limited number of agencies in the Inner Circle have acquired about the teaching related (classroom – oriented) aspects of English. Due to space limitations, we cannot list or elaborate upon all of the concerns here. Note, however, that these concerns are closely related to economic aspects, which we shall discuss below:

A list of such pedagogical concerns, includes, for example:

(a) the model for the teaching of English and its sociological and pragmatic validity;

(b) the band-wagons of methods, often commercially motivated, which seldom take into consideration the local needs and the various limitations in the Outer Circle;

(c) the teacher training programmes for ESL which have been developed in the Inner Circle for the training of "specialists";

(d) the fast-developing industry of tests for evaluating competence and proficiency in English and

(e) the approaches and research paradigms for English for Special Purposes (ESP)

These pedagogical aspects are just illustrative. One can add to that several other areas, for example, the pragmatic inadequacies of research on communicative competence, approaches to syllabus design, and research in applied lexicography.

The last aspect directly relates to economics: the economic motivations resulting in underlying conflicts. The economic aspects cannot be isolated from the other three aspects. However, the economic aspects do deserve highlighting since in recent years the economics of English has resulted in serious competition among the countries in the Inner Circle and the Outer Circle.

THE "KILLER" ENGLISH

This is a rather sensitive and complex issue. The use of linguistic power and politics invariably results in the suffering of language minorities and not uncommonly in the devouring of the smaller "linguistic fish" by a bigger "linguistic fish", a powerful language. This phenomenon has been described as "language death", "language attrition", "language shift", "lingocide", etc. The small "linguistic fish" refers to those languages which have a restricted number of speakers and/or limited depth and functional range.

In discussing language death, a distinction perhaps needs to be made between what one might call an inevitable language death and a death due to the motivated power (and politics) of another language. The ominous word "inevitable" here refers to the following:

(a) a demographically insignificant number of speakers;

(b) the pragmatically highly restricted domains of a language; and

(c) economic and social disadvantages of using a language.

The fundamental question appears to be: Has the international use of English become the main instrument of lingocide? One might also ask: what are the implications of the spread of English and its power on the rights of the speakers of minority and not-so-powerful / marginalised languages? We may consider here the illustrative cases of speakers of American

Indian languages, Australian Aboriginal languages, African and South Asian minority languages, among many others. The list can go on and on. The relationship between language and human rights has been very succinctly and exhaustively discussed in Philipson and Skutnab – Kangas's (1994) classic book, Linguistic Human Rights, which not only deals with theoretical aspects but also with case studies from different parts of the world and provides an excellent bibliography. Aggarwal (2000) has dealt with the problematic of language and human rights in India, with special reference to legal and constitutional provisions.

In a large number of studies, a direct case has been made blaming English for lingocide, language attrition and language death. We must realise, however, that the accusing finger cannot be pointed only at English for causing language death, for locally dominant and powerful Asian and African languages are also playing their roles in this lingocide and war of attrition. No doubt, the power and politics of English being immense in "depth" and "range", the implications are great. It is well documented by now that in the battle of languages, English has been the winner, certainly after World War II. As a consequence, it has left behind a trail of dead or dying languages, or languages which are not able to develop to their full potential in terms of gaining functional range.

THE POLITICS OF ENGLISH IN THE INNER CIRCLE

The Inner Circle is not free from this power struggle. Thus, the U.S.A., the United Kingdom, and to a lesser degree, Australia too, are competing with each other. The competition is, in many ways, to sell a particular model of English, to make a market for teachers (and "experts") from one's own country, to seek foreign students from a particular region of the world, and so on.

Achieving victory in the competition for selling a language and language – learning model has both material and strategic advantages. If a country outside the Inner Circle accepts a particular model of English, this naturally results in the creation of a market for pedagogical and technological materials, and equally important, for live human beings as "experts" and "products".

This rivalry among the cousins for selling a particular

method of teaching the language has also resulted in what one might call "linguistic paranoid". It is this feeling of paranoid that the Outer Circle is playing in turning the countries in the Inner Circle one against the other. Consider, as an example, the following observation of the British ESL expert Brumfit:

> There is already evidence that the varied sources of English are being exploited by countries in their attitudes to learning English. American English may be preferred to British by countries willing to express their independence from a traditional British connection: countries too closely connected by geography or history to the States have been known to turn towards Britain for a change in model and teaching policy for their English. Perhaps the same is happening in contact with Australia or New Zealand. The English – Speaking world can be played politically by the non-English speaking world. (1987:7)

One cannot fail to see this rivalry between the U.S.A. and the U.K. in the ESL – related professional organizations. However, on one point there seems to be an agreement, that is, to present a front of solidarity among the members of the Inner Circle. This is particularly true in the "international" organisations which claim to serve the cause of English internationally.

FOUCAULT'S APPROACH AND LINGUISTIC POWER

Let us go back now to our earlier mention of Foucault's insights on power, though, as we have already noted, his concerns are not specifically language related. In his view, power is interested in "relations", and language focuses "meaning". Even if we agree with this distinction, it seems that Foucault's discussion of various aspects and agencies of power, his conceptualisation of this phenomenon, and his insights concerning methodologies for understanding power, raise many language – related questions. One also finds many interesting parallels between issues which concern Foucault (e.g. the use of power by the state, or by the agencies of the state) and issues related to language, its manipulation abuse, codification, and so forth.

The language – related issues motivated by various types of power include, for example, first, the use of various types of manipulation for the spread of a language with the aim of gaining political, caste, economic, and class power. The goal of such application of power is to acquire control over a vital

aspect of human behaviour, language.

Second, we find the use of subtle or not-so-subtle linguistic devices for deception and propaganda – political, religious, commercial. It was due to this concern that a short-lived school of semantics developed after World War II. This concern is further evident in the current movement for "plain English", and in studies of the abuse of language in the media (e.g. see, Redish 1985 and Dayananda 1986 for discussion of Plain English and see relevant chapters in Bolinger 1980 regarding the media).

Foucault's "methodological precautions", briefly mentioned earlier, provide a useful framework for describing the power of language. Of course, Foucault provides only broad suggestions not specifically addressed to linguistic power. But language does not create power for itself; the agents of linguistic power are its promoters, and its users, who develop a power base for it. This is done by assigning "powerful" and significant roles for a language, by providing an important position to it in language planning (see, e.g. Aggarwal 1984), and by creating a context in which the user of the language acquires an attitudinal status.

In other words, the strategies for acquiring linguistic power have several similarities with other power acquiring strategies as for example, in politics. Thus, taking the five methodological guide-points of Foucault, one might rephrase his questions specifically with reference to the power of English. One has to, then, ask, for example:

1. What is the ultimate destination of the power of English?
2. Once the English knowing elite acquires the power of language at whatever level – what are their goals?
3. How has the network of the power of English been created?
4. Who are the agents who work within this network?
5. What kind of 'ideological change' does English produce?

The questions must be asked within the context of the international networks of English. The network had distinct characteristics within each Circle of English. The symbols of power, and the ultimate goals to be achieved, understandably,

differ within each Circle; they are often even in conflict with each other. The reality and the myth of the symbols have to be critically examined within each Circle. The Outer Circle is perceived to use the language for domination of various types – cultural, economic and political. It is seen, as the argument goes, to cause both conscious and unconscious lingocide and dislocation of native cultural traditions by introducing westernisation, albeit often under the garb of modernisation. This is the position taken by various groups and scholars in, for example, Iran, Pakistan, Nigeria and India. But, most importantly, English is seen as a tool of economic exploitation and political domination.

While this perception is by and large true, there is another side of the story too. The Outer Circle sees the other dimensions of the legacy of English, too: as a tool of national unity and integrity; of political awakening, a 'window on the world of knowledge', of advancement in sciences and technology, as a 'link' language – a tool to gloss over problems arising out of multilingualism and its concomitant language conflict and so on. The expanding circle, under the impact of the Internet and digital revolution, sees it as a vehicle for entering the 21st century.

It is interesting to note that English language has come to be characterized by an amazing variety of labels, labels that characterize power. Consider, for example, the following:

Labels use to Characterise Power of English

Positive	*Negative*
nationalunity and integrity	colonial legacy
literary renaissance	anti – nationalism
cultural mirror (for minority cultures)	anti – native culture materialism
modernisation	westernisation
liberalism	rootedlessness
universalism	loss of identity
technology	slavishness
science	ethnocentricism
mobility	permissiveness
access code	divisiveness alienation.

Often, the same term (e.g. westernisation) may be used in both in a positive and in a negative sense, depending on who uses it and for what purpose.

IDEOLOGY AND ENGLISH

The most important question Foucault asks is: what are the ideological products of power? To make this question appropriate to the purpose of this study, we shall ask: what kind of ideological change does English produce? Now, this naturally opens up the Pandora's Box and brings a host of questions. The answers depend on the shareholders' perception.

There is now a large body of literature – political, attitudinal, economic and of other genres – claiming that English is the most potent and powerful instrument of social, political and linguistic change. We will not discuss the issue of English and linguistic – literary change here. We however have seen in the foregoing section the different perceptions of English by various groups.

There is no doubt about the fact that a good deal of the current power English issues out of this multi-perception. Within each Circle, groups of various ideologies–the fundamentalists, the socialists, the nationalists, the humanists and so on–are exploiting the 'multisymbol' characteristics of English for their ulterior motives. Discussing this relationship between language and change, the famous Indian historian Panniker argues:

> Philosophy and religious thinking, however much they may influence the people in general, are the special interests of the intellectuals ...it is the change in the language that is in many ways the most far – reaching transformation in Asia, for it is not merely the reflection of the changed mind but is itself the instrument of continuing changes, for the new languages of Asia represent a new semantics, a new world of ideas and thought which is reaching a larger and larger circle every day (Panniker 1961: 329)

The power bases for English, then, have to be seen in both material and psychological terms. Note that there are several other accidental and not-so-accidental reasons which helped the Inner Circle to create a power base for English. In fact, the Inner Circle used both overt and covert strategies for the spread and power of English. One factor which contributed to the pluricentricity of English was the absence of an academy and a recognised codifying agency for English. One could only "revolt" against an organised body with the mission of codification, but,

as we know, for English there was no such organized academy. The most subtle strategy adopted was "psychological bar", which is effective and, at the same time, elusive. This is true in the Inner Circle as well as in the Outer Circle.

In psychological terms, English now has support groups in the Outer Circle which have given it credit for cultural renaissance, spread of nationalism (in the classical European sense), pan – regional literary creativity, and neutrality. It is due to these psychological reasons that there is a strong emotional attachment to the language. This type of attachment is unprecedented in the history of language spread. It is interesting that the native speakers of English in the Inner Circle have as yet not recognized this psychological factor.

A total profile of the present power of English cannot underplay the psychological factors. These factors are vital for creating an "identity" with the language and for contributing to the belief in the "alchemy" of English (Kachru 1986) or functionally considering it a "language for all seasons / reasons". What we need, then, is to develop typologies for the power and politics of English for the three Circles. It is through such typologies that one can understand the current power and politics of English, and its effects and consequences on different societies and cultures.

On the whole, the present study raises questions and does not necessarily provide answers. Concerning the global functioning of English, as yet not many meaningful questions have been asked. It is not that one does not think of such questions since most of these are rather obvious. It seems that in the suppression of such questions, if one examines carefully and critically, we might find an interplay of "power" and "politics". Much more importantly, perhaps, local, empirical questions need to be asked pointedly with regard to the power and politics of English. Regrettably, barring a few exceptions, this topic has not been addressed seriously in the academic constituency, even though in the media and political discourse it has received some attention, opportunistic and otherwise. The present study proposes to make some advance on the topic, by raising some empirical questions and combining social, economic political and historical material on the power and politics of English in north-east India, with special reference to Manipuri and Assamese native speakers.

2

LOCATING THE STUDY: THE NORTH-EAST SCENARIO: A REVIEW OF SOCIOLINGUISTICS AND ELT CONTEXTS

The North-east Scenario

North-east India stands out for its unique ethnic, cultural, linguistic, and religious diversity not to be found in any other region of country. A large number of ethnic groups and Scheduled Tribes, with different religions and sects, speaking virtually one-fourth of the languages spoken in the country inhabit the region. Additionally, the strong impact of typographical features on identity formation have multiplied the heterogeneous composition of this region (Karna 1999:31)

The ethnic heterogeneity of the region unfolds a complexity based on distinctive historical experiences. Out of the seven states, as many as four – Arunachal Pradesh, Meghalaya, Mizoram and Nagaland – are not only tribal majority states (nearly 95+ percent of the populations in these states are Scheduled Tribes), but their history, culture and economy have features remarkably different from the tribal pockets elsewhere in the country. The three other states – Assam, Manipur and Tripura – have a majority of non-tribal plains population, but even in these states the tribal population (varying from about 16% to 36%) is substantially higher than the national average.

Compared to other parts of the country, the colonial incorporation of the north–east started much later. While Manipur

and Tripura were independent principalities maintaining relations with the British since the late eighteenth century, the colonial rulers annexed Assam in 1826 and subsequently the Naga, Mizo, Khasi, Jaintia and Garo Hills. The North – East Frontier Area (NEFA, now Arunachal Pradesh) came under colonial control in the second half of the nineteenth century. Under the colonial dispensation, certain areas were either 'excluded' or 'partially excluded' from the purview of the then prevailing administrative and statutory controls, allowing the people to maintain their customary control over load and forests. However, attempts were simultaneously made to exploit the natural resources by establishing links with the process operating outside the region. Further, the extension of market links, introduction of money, entry of government officials, traders, moneylenders and shop keepers created a situation under which vested interests from outside could grab land through control and alienation. The plain areas, primarily inhabited by non-tribal indigenous communities, were brought under the revenue arrangements that were prevailing in other parts of British India (*ibid*: 32)

The situation started changing swiftly after Assam was opened up for tea plantation by the middle of the nineteenth century. Afterwards, exploitation of natural oil, coal mines and forests developed at full speed. Such changes in economic activities brought a large number of immigrant labour to the region. While agriculture was almost stagnant due to the slow growth of indigenous population, new economic activities absorbed mainly outsiders. Under the circumstances, indigenous people's control over local resources began to decline. Simultaneously, the arrival of Christian missionaries and the spread of Christianity in tribal areas in the later part of the nineteenth century not only introduced organised religion, but brought about changes in the social life of the people. Perhaps, the most significant development during this period was the emergence of an educated, modernized elite. The constitutional developments during the 1920's and 1930's synchronised with the growing political and ethno-linguistic consciousness in the region. The government of India Act of 1919 provided for declaring tribal area as '**backward**

tract' and the Act of 1935 as **'excluded areas or partially excluded areas**. Only some selected areas were allowed to send representatives to the Provincial Legislature before 1947. The attempt to turn the North-East region into an independent political entity separate from India under the Coupland Plan failed on the eve of independence (*ibid*:33)

Not only did the colonial administrators, but politicians, media personnel and even social scientists in the post independent era love, by and large, have accepted the **North–East** as an undifferentiated category. To support this notion, they attribute some commonness to it, the most important of which are:

1. All the north-eastern states are economically backward.
2. The people of the seven states suffer from utter deprivation.
3. All communities, small or large, of the region are assertive as to their affinity and apprehensive of the loss of their identity.
4. Most of the communities, at present, are highly restive and from amongst them insurgent outfits have emerged with the primary objective of 'liberating' themselves from what they call 'Indian Domination'.

However, recently certain scholars have taken exceptions to this undifferentiated catergorisation, emphasising both commonalities and individualities among the groups, communities and states in the region. Choudhury states: "Even a casual scrutiny of the north-east societies would reveal that different ethnic groups of the region differ from one another significantly so as to their material advancement, cultural attainments, social mobility and perception of Indianness" (1991:91). We cannot go into the details of the similarities and difference among all the communities and all the states. We will discuss very briefly the plains Assamese and plains Manipuri cases, the main concerns of the present study.

The Assamese is the most Sanskritised community of the north-east, which speaks an Indo-Aryan language and has a developed literature. As per recorded evidence, Sankritisation

of western Assam started as early as the fifth century AD and the process was extended to the eastern frontier of Assam not later than the nineteenth century AD. The Assamese people inhabiting the Brahmaputra valley responded favourably to all pan–Indian social and cultural movements. In the sixteenth century, the emergence of the Vaisnavite saint, Shankardeva, marked the completion of the process of Sanskritisation of Assam. The Assamese elite that emerged during the colonial period (due to English education among other things) participated in the early Congress Session. Since 1921, Assamese people from all walks of life contributed substantially to the Indian Freedom struggle, responding spontaneously to Gandhiji's call. One can clearly surmise that the Indianness of the Assameese people has had been a growth from within, through prolonged historical, social, political, cultural and economic interaction of more than fifteen hundred years. "Secessionism, propagated by the United Liberation Front of Assam (ULFA), is a very recent phenomenon in Assam and it emerged as a by-product of the Assam agitation [ethnic Assamese movement coupled with anti-immigrant / anti-foreigner riots] launched in 1979" (*ibid*: 92).

The case of Manipuris inhabiting the Valley/plains is quite different and quite complicated. These Manipuris, till around the 1960s, used to draw inspiration from the Sanskritised culture since the eighteenth century, during which period they were converted to Hinduism under royal patronage, and to which they have made meaningful contribution. But, in the last four decades or so, there has been a marked qualitative transformation in subjective perception and the objective situation. Surrounded by the Naga, Kuki and other tribes in the Hills, the Manipuris seem perpetually apprehensive of the tribal assertions. Further, the overt Sanskritised way of life and identification with the Indian mainstream by certain sections of Manipuris has come under serious scrutiny by the different valley based insurgent groups.

Being an erstwhile princely state, the aristocracy of Manipur valley has been a well–entrenched privileged minority and which maintained its position by joining the Congress after Independence.

Interestingly, a form of communist / socialist movement, launched by the Manipuri national hero, Jananeta Irabot Singh, marks an ironical link with mainstream India. More recently a breach with Hinduism–coupled with the Mongoloid origin of the ethnic group, its language and the emphasis on the return to its indigenous religion, i.e. 'Sanamahism' – has been made a component of the militant–secessionist struggle. Apparently, the secessionist threat of Manipur is more serious than that of Assam, though some would propose that in the long run it would continue only as a bargaining monoeuvre as in Assam.

MANIPUR: THE PLACE, PEOPLE AND THEIR HISTORY

Manipur, described as the 'Switzerland of the East' by Lord Irwin and a 'Jewel of India' by Pundit Jawaharlal Nehru, is a veritable 'little paradise on earth' on the easternmost corner of India. Today, Manipur evokes a kind of ambivalent attitude. On the one hand, it is a rich museum of diverse people belonging to different racial, ethnic, linguistic and religious groups offering great attraction. The dress, food habits, dances, handicrafts, games, sports, performing arts, the flora and the fauna, among others, makes it tremendously fascinating. On the other hand, various forms of social movements, viz. the Kuki Rebellion, the Zeliangrong Uprising, the Nupi Lal (Women's War) and virtually every day reports of ethnic strife and underground movements, of insurgency and AIDS pandemic evoke a kind of awe and fear (cf. Aggarwal 1994), Any single narrative of the past and present of the people and the place would be utterly inadequate. Yet, we present brief account as a backgrounder.

The Origin and Composition of Manipuri Society

Manipur is bounded on the north-west by Nagaland, by the cachar district of Assam on the west, by Mizoram on the south-west and by Myanmar on the South-East. The tiny border state is dominated by thickly forested high hills which cover about 90% (20,089 sq.kms) of the total area of the state, though only about one-third of the state'' total population live in them. These hills encircle the oval shaped fertile alluvial plains (2,238 sq. kms.) of Manipur Valley, with Imphal, the state capital at the centre.

The state is divided into eight revenue districts, three of which are located in the valley (Imphal, Bishnupur, Thoubal) and the other five are hill districts (Senapati, Ukhrul, Tamenglong, Churachandpur and Chandel). Our chief concern here is with the three valley districts where the Manipuri or Meetei Hindus live.

The early geopolitical boundary of the state fluctuated considerably in a number of historical epochs. The present political boundary became a reality after several compromises and treaties with the rulers of Burma and Cachar during the British regime. Being an important land route for trade and commerce for China and the Far East Asia, with the Near East and Middle East, Manipur was known by different names to peoples of different countries, viz. Poirei, Meiteileipak, Kangleileipak, Mekhala, Meckley, among a host of others.

Imphal is the only 'City' in the state, centrally located in the central Valley of Manipur. Given the unique pattern of the geo-political peopling in the state, Imphal cannot claim to represent the composite culture of Manipur. No doubt, it is the prime seat of political and economic activities of the state. Socio-culturally, however, it is the centre of all activities and institutions for the overwhelmingly majority Meetei population. Imphal was a class II town in 1961 with a population of 67,717 persons. While Imphal remains the only city in the state with 1,00,000+ population, in the 1991 census a distinction has been made between "Imphal Urban Agglomeration" with a total population of 2,00,615 persons and "Imphal Municipality" with 1,96,268 persons as inhabitants. The absolute figures for total literates in Imphal Urban Agglomeration and Imphal Municipality have been given as 1,43,946 (83,067 males and 60,633 females) persons respectively (*Census of India*: Series 15 – Manpower Paper-1991)

The inhabitants of Imphal city may be divided into the following six groups: (1) Meeteis – the overwhelmingly dominant, majority population of the state; (ii) the Bamons or Brahmins; (iii) Pangans or the Manipuri Muslims; (iv) the Lois (Scheduled Castes); (v) Hills people (Scheduled Tribes); and, (vi) Mayangs, meaning outsiders referring to the more recent immigrant

communities from the Indian mainstream (cf. Promodini 1989) For the specific purposes of the present study, we will only provide a brief outline of the meeteis community.

The Manipuri-Meeteis

A great deal of confusion exists with regard to the origin of the Meeteis. While some claim the identity of the present Manipur state with the one mentioned in the Hindu epic, The *Mahabharata*, others call it simply an 'Indian fallacy'. Historians of repute, like R.C. Mazumdar, while recognising the multi-racial, multi-ethnic, multi-cultured and diverse historical origin and reality of the people of India, and, by implication, of the existence of non-Aryan peoples and cultures in the ancient subcontinent, betray an Aryanization zeal as far as Manipur is concerned. On the one hand, Mazumdar (1968:50) testifies that different people belonging to different races and cultures did exist in the pre-Aryan period: "In the first place, there is no historical basis for the popular belief that the peoples, of Manipur had no culture worth the name until the Aryan came and civilized them". Chatterjee (1960) corroborates this point of view as he states, ".... when the Aryans came into India, the country was not a no-man's land–it was already populated by some races and peoples who had risen to a high level of civilization." But, as one comes to specific societies, as we will see in the case of Manipuris, most of these scholar-historians tend to take an absolute Aryan, Hindu view.

A number of material and cultural achievements of the Meetei people in the ancient period, as recorded in different old manuscripts, have been cited as evidence to support the claim of a developed civilization in the Manipur Kingdom. The use of metals and coins, trade in silk, tea, and other products, a self-sufficient economy, statecraft and an organised defense force, a distinctive script and literature and the like have been found recorded in about a thousand old Meeteis manuscripts (cf. Sanajaoba 1991). In sharp contrast to several archaeological, paleographic, philological, anthropological and folk evidences (cf. Kabui 1991), scholars like Menon (1956) consider the early history of Manipur as obscure. In fact, Chatterjee (1974) regrets

this bias and states that most Indian historians had neglected the achievements of the people of Mongoloid origin in Indian historiography.

Thus, while many Indian as well as Meetei scholars have boldly advanced arguments such as that the Meeteis are Hindus, that the present day Manipur is the Manipur of *Mahabharata*, that the Meetei alphabets have been derived from the Nagari and Bengali scripts, a recent section of influential Meetei intelligentsia claims a closer racial and cultural affinity with the present day South-East and Far East Asia. They emphasize their Mongoloid origin, while recognising the fact that, in course of time, they have assimilated features of other racial categories (cf. Sanajaoba 1991). Grierson (1904) traces the origin of the Meeteis from the upper courses of the Yangtze and the Hoyang-Ho rivers in China. Johnstone (1971: 97) concludes, "The Manipuries themselves are a fine stalwart race descended from an Indo-Chinese stock with some admixture of Aryan blood, derived from the successive waves of Aryan invaders that have passed through the valley in pre-historic days." Pemberton (1835) thinks that "... the Manipuries of the present day are the descendents of the Tartar colony which probably emigrated from the North-West borders of China...". It may be noted here that wet rice cultivation, domestication of animals like the ox and buffalo, use of metals like bronze and iron, matriarchy, high social status of women, and a complex of belief systems of animism, ancestor worship and reverence for high status people and places are some of the material and sociocultural features that the Meeteis share with the South-East Asian peoples.

Formation of the Meetei Ethnic Group

The integration of seven major clans and principalities (viz. Angom, Khaba, Nongchup, Chenglei, Khuman, Luwang and Ningthouja) led to the development of a common Meetei ethnic group as also of the Manipuri Kingdom in the ancient period (cf. Yumjao 1966). During the medieval period, immigrants like the Brahmins from northern India, Muslims from Cachar and the Mayangs, after inter-marriage with native Meeteis (mostly women) and assimilating Manipuri language and cultural

characteristics became part of the Meetei community.

It is worth pointing out here that there was no social stratification like the Hindu *Varna* system in the Meetei community before its Hinduisatian. Secondly, the Hindu-Muslim communal divide was and has been totally non-existent. In fact, ironically enough, king Pamheiba (1709-1798) of Manipur, who was the first Meetei King to adopt Hinduism as the royal religion, was rechristened as King Gharib Newaj, an Urdu name (cf. Aggarwal 1994). Lastly, the Mayangs of the medieval period were quite different from the 20th century (immigrant) Mayangs. In the medieval period, the Bengali and Tripuri immigrants were referred to as Mayangs, even after their assimilation into the Meetei community. Now while these Mayangs prefer to call themselves Meeteis, the Meeteis prefer to call them the Vishnupuriyas (cf. Manihar 1987). The present day Mayangs, however, are mainstream Indian people who, by and large, are on the peripheries of Meetei ethnic group.

Manipur since Ancient times

Some of the ancient Meetei texts, provide useful insights into the material, political, social and cultural characteristics of the early Meetei people. For example, the Meeteilon literary classic, *Poireiton Khunthok,* available in the different renditions (Chandra Singh 1979 and Yaima Singh 1971) provides accounts of the use of metals like gold, silver, iron and bell metal, the use of fire, the techniques of weaving, paddy cultivation, and the use of bows for hunting, among other things. They also mention the prevalence of socio-cultural practices like cremation of the dead, polyandry, frequent divorces, sacrifices of animals and offer of wine for friendship.

Another important classic, *Cheitharol Kumbabha,* "The Royal Chronicle" (Khelchandra and Ibungohal 1967) reveals the nature of the polity and affairs of state during the rule of the Meetei kings. It corroborates the claim of historians (cf. Kabui 1991) that a prototype of a constitution had come into being in Manipur in 429 A.D. Later, King Loiyumba Shinyen (1074-1112) described the duties and responsibilities/obligations of the Meetei King and the different employees in the Kingdom as well as the

details of the network of administration. The administration was carried out by a council of 10 cabinet ministers, known as 'Pangda Tara'. In addition, there were 64 high lords representing the 32 administrative units of the Kingdom. The principle followed was, as expressed in the local proverb 'Leibakna Nama', meaning one part by the people and another by the King. Apart from the royal chronicle, the 'maichous' (private scholars of eminence) maintained records of state administration, including private affairs of the members of the royal family.

Many of the early Manipuri/Meeteilon manuscripts, estimated to exceed one thousand, preserved over generations in the personal custody of the 'maichous', have been rendered into modern Manipuri in the second half of the twentieth century. These manuscripts cover areas like administration, arts & culture, astrology, charms and 'mantras', health and hygine, genealogy, creation myths, geography, geology, religious and moral philosophy etc. (cf. Khelchandra 1984). Commenting on the Meetei's literary achievements in older times, Chatterjee writes, "Manipuri literature is most emphatically an advanced modern Indian literature, and cannot be described as the backward literature of the so called Adivasi and primitive people, the Manipuri writers are already in the frontline of modern Indian writing and translation" (1974).

Studies of Meetei numismatics reveal that Meetei coins were in use from 568-658 A.D. till 1891 A.D. (cf. Yumjao Singh 1966). Hodson (1908) records, "I have before me now eight varieties of Sel coins, dating from the reign of Pakungba [Pakhangba] downwards". Due to economic prosperity of Manipur Kingdom, it was regularly attacked by the Burmese. Harassed and humiliated by these Burmese incursions, the King of Manipur signed a friendship treaty with the British rulers in India in September 1762, with an assurance to pay hundred gold and silver coins and other precious goods in return for the British safeguard against Burmese aggression (cf. Kabui 1991). This testifies to the existence of a monetised economy.

Since the early times, the Meeteis have also developed a variety of games, sports and martial arts among a host of other

performing and physical arts. Many of the Meetei indigenous games like 'Boat Race', 'Mukna' (a local version of rugby), and 'polo' may be considered unique requiring high mental and physical discipline and moral codes.

Women have occupied a unique place throughout history in the Meetei social structure. They had separate family courts, separate women's market, a higher degree of economic and political independence and even the prerogative to move the King to alter his decision by collective appeal. The women of Manipur have been very industrious – the entire management of the internal trade and exchange of the produce of Manipur Kingdom depends(ed) on them. On the contrary, the male population has developed a number of unproductive habits like indulgence in cock-fighting, gambling, non-payment of debts, among a host of others (cf. Sanajaoba 1991: 41).

The Advent of Hinduism

Before the imposition of Hinduism, the Meeteis had their traditional religion, which included total faith in the highest local deity Lord Sanamahi homage to 'Paphal' (a posture of a coiled serpent symbolising cosmic order), and a number of rituals and festivals. The 'paphal' has more than 300 forms. Refuting the Aryan or Hindu origin of the Meeteis, several scholars argue that while many of the Hindu religious texts opened with a curse on the serpent, serpent-worship, which is essentially a Turanian practice, by the Meeteis indicates their non-Aryan, non-Hindu origin (cf. Ferguson 1971). The Meeteis were and are highly ritualistic people, which has led several scholars to characterize Manipur as a ritual theatre state (cf. Arambam 1991). Brown (1873) observes, "In their intercourse among themselves, the Manipuries are ceremonious. They address one another by the name of the office they may hold, or as younger or elder brother. To call a man 'Angang' (literally meaning a child among other symonyms) is most respectful...".

Charairongba (1967-1709) was the first King of Manipur who adopted Hinduism of the Krishna cult. But he made no attempt to make it a state religion. The major religious change

took place during the reign of King Garib Newaz (1707-1748). In 1717, he was initiated into Hinduism of the Rama cult of Vaishnavism by Santi Das Gosai, a Hindu Brahmin from Sylhet (in Bangladesh now). Then, the King, under total control of Hindu Brahmins, took up a series of measures to annihilate the traditional religion. In 1723, all the temples of the Meetei lais (local high deities) were pulled down (cf. Khelchandra 1969). Thus by a process of syncretism, the Meetei pantheon, deities and holy places were renamed. Even the seven 'Yeks' (clans) of the Meetei community were identified with the 'gotras' of the Hindus viz. Mangan → Shandillya; Luwang → Kashyas; Khuman → Modhugalya, Angan → Gautam Bharadwaja, and Chinglei → Vashistha. The biggest bell metal image of Lord Sanamahi was destroyed in 1726. In 1727, all the 'maichous' were forced to bring all books in their possession and these manuscripts numbering about 120, written in the archaic Meetei script, on different subjects like culture, religion, history, politics etc, were put on a funeral pyre and burnt to ashes in an event popularly known as *Puya Meithaba.* A strict royal edict was proclaimed not to sing devotional songs in Manipuri. Any one found reading, writing or speaking in the old Manipuri was executed (cf. Aggarwal 1992). Hudson, in the beginning of the century, commented: "Religious dissent was treated with the same ruthless severity as meted out to political opponents, and wholesale banishment, and execution drove the people into acceptance of the tenets of Hinduism."(1908).

The zenith of the spread and transplantation of Hindu Vaishnavite cult and culture came during the reign of King Bhagyachandra (1759-1798), the grandson of King Garib Newaz. He carved a huge image of Lord Govinda out of a tree in 1780 and introduced the 'Rasa' (Hindu classical) dance.

Hinduism got still a further boost during the reign of King Churachand (1891-1941) who created one hundred posts in the Brahma Sabha, the seat of religious administration in Manipur. Ojha P. Atombapu Sharma, a scholar attached to the royalty, wrote about 100 monographs in English, during this period, to provide justification for the Aryanization and Hinduisation of the Meeteis.

Thus the period from the reign of King Garib Newaz to that of Churachand was a period of near absolute transformation of the socio-religious life of the Meeteis, increasingly called the Manipuris. Not only traditional gods and goddesses were identified with those of the Hindu pantheon, but even lakes, rivers, hills etc. were given Sanskrit names (cf. Yumjao 1966). Further, during the period, a "clean-unclean' controversy, locally known as 'Mangba-Sengba', was given patronage by the royal court. People who opposed Hinduism were ostracized an entire family or a whole village was declared 'unclean'. Only after they paid a penalty they were admitted to the Hindu fold.

In spite of all this, Hinduism has not succeeded in either totally destroying the traditional religion of the Meeteis, known as Sanamahism, or in penetrating deep into the lives of large sections of people in general. In fact, the impact of Hinduism has only been superficial. "Hinduism has left its mark in ritual pollution, ceremonial elaborations and purification, outward manifestation of religious devoutness, but the overall effect is only marginal" (Das 1985:5). McCulloch, who spent about 27 years in Manipur, writes: "But although they [Meeteis] thus profess Hindooism, they have not given up their ancient worship and above three hundred deities are still propitiated by appropriate sacrifice of things abhorent to real Hindus"(1957:92).

In recent decades, a religious movement, centering round Sanamahism, has been started by the Meetei youth and various organisations, with the following basic objectives, among others:

i) to renounce Hinduism

ii) to discard all claims of Sanskritisatian invented by the Hindu scholars; and

iii) to take up necessary measures for the revival of Meetei traditional religion, culture, script, language, literature and develop them to meet the modern needs.

During the 70s of the last century, the movement gained its strength. The major objectives during this period included:

i) observation of Condolence Day of "Puya Meithaba" on the 21st of January every year;

ii) non-observance of Saraswati Puja in educational institutions

iii) Revival of the Meetei language and script etc.

Since the 1980s, the movement has acquired serious dimensions as it has become complicated with the underground secessionist movements (cf. Nilabir 1991).

Manipuri Language and Script

Manipuri language, or Meeteilon as it is named by the native speakers, has been described in the Census of India reports since 1881. Grierson (1904) in his *Linguistic Survey of India* (Vol. III, Part III), classified Meeteilon under the Kuki-Chin group of the Tibeto-Burman language sub-family, although for the lack of adequate philological and synchronic information on Meeteilon and on finding an apparent gulf between Meeteilon and other languages of the Kuki-Chin group, he considered 'Meetei-Chin' as the more appropriate name. Grierson and his associates found that Meeteilon sometimes agreed more closely with Burmese and even with Tibetan than the Kuki-Chin languages proper (*ibid*). Later, as a result of good deal of contrastive studies on Tibeto-Burman languages, it was suggested that there were predominant affinities between Meeteilon and Kuki-Naga (cf. Benedict 1972).

The subjection of the Meeteis to Hinduism brought about significant linguistic changes in Meeteilon, or Manipuri language. It was not simply a question of introducing certain Sanskrit and Bengali vocabulary items and the replacement of the age-old Meetei script by Bengali script, but the very character of the developed literary language was threatened (cf. Aggarwal 1991). Sarmah (1965) laments, "The cruel design of history and the grievance of our language lie in the abolition of centuries old Meetei language and supplantation [cf. the old script] by Bengali script, which is not adequate enough to meet the needs of our mother tongue. As a result of the inbuilt weakness of Bengali script to carry the burden of Meetei language, disadvantage and devastation had been witnessed; Meetei books written in Bengali script create chaos in the field of spelling, punctuation and tonal variation."

There has been a great deal of controversy with regard to the origin and development of the old, indigenous Meetei script (cf. Aggarwal 1993). The most commonly accepted version is that it evolved during the reign of King Kiyamba (1469-1503 A.D.). This has been corroborated by studies of stone inscriptions as well as epigraphic and numismatic studies, apart from the studies of old manuscripts. There are other versions as well (see for example, Grierson 1904, Damant 1877, among others), but we will restrict our discussion of this aspect here.

What is of utmost importance to the present study is that it is not the formal linguistic concerns but concerns of ethnolinguistic identity that have become closely associated with matters relating to Manipuri language, literature, and script. Commenting on the intimate link between religion and script, Chatterji writes: "From the time of King Garib Newaz Singh of Manipur (1709-1748), the Manipuri people, through the influence of the Bengali Vaishnava of Chaitanya School from Nawadip and Sylhet, accepted the Bengali script for their language (C.1740) and now this has become fully established" ('1971:18). Again, this view does not hold water in view of the fact that the movement to restore the original Meetei script had already started by then and the decision for its revival was taken to the floor of the Manipur Legislative Assembly by 1978 (cf. Aggarwal 1991).

Modern Immigration

From the beginning of the 18th century, there was continuous inflow of immigrants, both Hindus and Muslims, to Manipur. The successive Manipuri Kings allowed the immigrants to take Meetei wives as also to possess land for agriculture and other activities. Thus all immigrants, then, were called 'Nagangs' except the Brahmins and Muslims (cf. Manihar 1987). The Muslims were brought to Manipur as 'prisoners of war' or 'captives', but were later allowed to settle in the sparsely populated Kingdom. Apart from being allowed to marry Meetei women and occupy land for cultivation, they were assigned duties like weaving, metal work, bugle playing and defense services. The Brahmins, of course, were assigned with priestly and other religious work. In course of time, after several generations of settlement, the

Muslims, locally known as 'Meetei Pangans' and the Brahmins, called 'Meetei Bamons' by and large got assimilated into the Meetei community. No doubt, "Kingship was instrumental in Meetei identity conferment to the immigrants"(Lokendrajit 1986:346). The Meetei Pangans and Bamons have literally abandoned their ancestral languages and adopted Manipuri as their mother tongue.

More recently, however, the term 'Mayang' has come to refer to immigrants from different mainstream Indian States. Many of them were Bengalis who have had some English education and were brought to Imphal under the directive of the Political Agent in order to perform official duties. Then came the people from Cachar and Marwaris from north Indian states. The Punjabis, as a trading community, represent the latest arrivals. There are also people from Bihar, Uttar Pradesh, Orissa etc. who are engaged either in small business or provide services as barbers, cobblers, washermen, or simply unskilled menial workers. Most of these people came under the patronage of the Meetei Kings (cf. Kabui 1975:1). These different mainstream communities have mostly settled in the urban areas of Imphal Valley. Their presence in the rural areas of the valley or in the hills is negligible.

In contrast to the earlier immigrants, the recent immigrants to Imphal from other Indian states have not assimilated into the local community. Lokendrajit (1986:346) explains the causes thus, "influx of population now is inversely proportionate to the non-functioning of the assimilation mechanism." These Nayangs' or 'Outsiders' can be divided into relatively 'permanent residents' and the 'floating population', both contributing to significant changes in the ethnolinguistic and demographic composition of Manipur valley.

The present context of Imphal

During the half-a-century following the 'political' independence of India, there has been a sea-change in the political, social, economic, ethnolinguistic and cultural conditions of Manipur. In fact, unlike other north-eastern states, but similar (not identical though) to the Brahmaputra Valley Manipur

constituted an independent Kingdom or principality since the beginning of known history. After independence, it became a constitutional monarchy in 1948 with its own Legislative Assembly. However, under the recommendations of the States Reorganisation Commission, 1956, Manipur was made a Union Territory, thereby coming under the direct administration of the Central government of India. Opposition grew to this arrangement, and repeated demands for full statehood within the Indian Union were recognised when Manipur was converted to a separate state in 1972.

In Manipur, as in other states of North-East India, the dynamics of Identity and intergroup relations basically depend on the ethnicity of the groups involved. The reorganisation of states in this area on ethnic basis, as opposed to the linguistic principle in the case of rest of India, is a clear reflection of the paramount importance of ethnic group and identity in the area. Ethno-linguistic, political, and cultural mobilization and movements launched by various ethnic groups in the region remain ongoing processes. In most cases the attempts have been to highlight only one dimension of the problem, viz. the 'insiders' perspective or the 'outsiders' perspective, or the 'plains' vs. 'hills' people's perspectives. For example, many scholars have stated that, in Manipur, the basic problems relate for the dominance of the comparatively better off, numerically majority and politically powerful plains people trying to subjugate the tribal. At the same time, sections of tribal elite have been trying to assert and reassert their identity for a fair deal (cf. Das 1989:247). Thus the major problems in the state, which mostly find their ethnolinguistic, social, cultural and political manifestations and expressions in the capital city of Imphal relate to the relations between the three significant groups, viz. Meeteis, outsiders and tribals.

It has been repeatedly asserted by Meetei ethnic leaders as well as scholars that the Meetei community is basically classless and casteless (cf. Sanajaoba 1991). However, such a hypothesis has been proved invalid by the works of several social scientists, both linguists and non-linguists. Some scholars, for example, state that while there was no caste system in Manipur in the

pre-Hinduisation period, there certainly was some sort of class system (cf. Singh 1978). Promodini (1989) finds differences in the use of kinship and address terms between social groups like the 'RKs' (or Rajkumars, who are the descendents of the male members of the royal family), the 'loymas' (the descendents of the female members of the royal family), the 'Meetei Hao Aranba' (meaning 'commoners'), the Lois and Yaithibis (both Scheduled castes) and the like. These certainly reflect a kind of socio-cultural stratification in pre-Hinduisation Meetei society.

After conversion to Hinduism, there certainly has emerged a kind of caste system which, of course, is not as rigid as in mainstream India. Clearly, a structure of ranked hierarchy has emerged (cf. Promodini 1989). The Brahmins and the Meeteis, for example, do not accept cooked food or water from the remaining groups as they are considered to be of low status. Again, a Brahmin can have hypergamic relationship with Meeteis by marrying a Meetei woman, but he maintains his ritual, hierarchical distance from his wife by not accepting food cooked by her. Still another example is that of Lois. They originally belonged to the Meetei community but lived in geographically isolated villages. After the emergence of Hinduism, these people were ex-communicated from the Meetei ethnic group for various political and cultural reasons. They were branded 'Lois" which has derogatory socio-cultural connotations.

As already pointed out, the different tribal communities in Manipur have been broadly classified into two broad groups – the Nagas and the Kukis. However, within each group, there are different communities with different ethnolinguistic and socio-politico-cultural features. Further, one can notice the emergence of new groups claiming distinct identity like the Lushais (cf. Gangte 1984) and the Zeliangrongs (cf. Joykumar 1993).

This backgrounder to the Manipur Valley will help us, as well shall see in the following chapters, gain better insights into the power and politics of English in the sociolinguistic setting of Manipur.

ASSAM: THE PLACE, PEOPLE AND THEIR HISTORY

Assam commands a unique place in the North-eastern region of India. It is situated between 24 and 28 degrees of north latitude, and between 89 and 97 degrees of east longitude. This largest north-east state encompasses two valleys, viz. the Brahmaputra Valley and the Barak (Surma) Valley, alongwith large central and north-eastern hill tracts. The Assamese-Ahoms inhabit the Brahmaputra Valley, the heartland of Assam and the focus of our study. Blessed with rich alluvial soil, the valley comprises a vast land of 30,000 square miles, beginning from Manal River on the north bank of river Brahmaputra to the foot of the Himalayas close upon the frontiers of China. On the north, it is bounded by the hills occupied by SC and ST communities such as Bhutias, Akas, Duflas, Abors and Miris; on the north-east, the Mishmi hills sweep round the head of the valley. The hills inhabited by the Khomtis and the Singphos separate Assam from China and Burma. On the south, the so-called Assam Range is occupied by the Nagas, Jaintias and Khasis, while Garos inhabit the hills westward.

Girted thus almost on all sides by mountain barriers, Assam practically remained isolated. Outsiders seldom appeared on her soil, while few from Assam crossed its boundary. Although the river Brahmaputra formed the highway of communication, navigation along the river, before steam-engines came, was always extremely hazardous, even fatal. Thus, geography had imposed a formidable barrier in Assam's contact with the rest of the world. However, through numerous passes and river routes, it was accessible to the hills and vice-versa.

Apart from its rich green, fresh and cool landscape, Assam is rich in natural resources. The mountains contain mines of coal, limestone and iron-ores, the rivers abound in gold dust. The rich alluvial soil is well-suited for all kinds of agricultural purposes so that it might be converted into a continuous garden of silk, cotton, sugar, tea and coffee, apart from rice.

The Origin and Composition of Assamese Society

There are numerous myths about the origin of the Assamese

people. While some connect them to Lord Vishnu, others trace them to some characters in the Hindu epic, *The Mahabharata*. These myths are so discordant, unconvincing and confusing that most modern scholars, including the native intelligentsia have abandoned them. Perhaps the most convincing and widely accepted version is the formation of a Kingdom under Ahom rulers.

The Ahom Kingdom, best described as the cultural heartland of modern Assam, came under British rule in 1826, when, according to the Yandabo Treaty that ended the Anglo-Burmese war, the King of Ava (Burma) renounced "all claim upon" Assam and agreed to "abstain from all future interferences with the principality of Assam and its dependencies, and also with the contiguous petty state, of Cachar and Jyntea" [Jaintia] ('Treaty of Yandabo', in Bose, ed. 1979; 61-62). As pointed out earlier, towards the end of the eighteenth century, the expanding Burmese empire had began to interfere in the affairs of the Ahom, Manipur and other small kingdoms in northeast India. Internal dissension within the Ahom court as well as the King's family had led to dissident factions cultivating ties with the Burmese court. Starting in 1817, there were a number of Burmese military invasions of Assam. In 1822, the Ahom kingdom came to be ruled by a Burmese commander. The Ahom aristocracy escaped to British territories and sought British help against the Burmese invaders. As the East India Company's territories came to border the Burmese empire, the latter's military incursions began to alarm the British, making for a convergence of interests between the Assamese and East India Company against the Burmese.

When the Ahom Kingdom passed into British hands, it was the first time in history that the Assamese heartland became politically incorporated into a pan-Indian imperial formation. The Ahoms had successfully resisted the Mughals, but for very brief period of subjugation. There were serious conflicts between the Ahom Kingdom and the Mughals in the seventeenth century, and in 1662 the Mughal General Mirjumla blitzed through Assam and plundered the capital city of Gargaon. But this period of conflict ended with the Ahom army defeating the Mughals in

1682. Having said this much, we will talk about the composition of present day Assamese society a little later.

The Assamese-Ahoms

The history of the Ahom Kingdom, however, is not synonymous with the area that came to be referred to as Assam, Assam as a colonial province – a chief commissionership to be exact – was formed in 1874. Prior to that the British ruled Assam as an "appendage of the unwieldy province of Bengal"(Gait 1990: 336). The new province initially included the (undivided) districts of Goalpara, Kamrup, Darrang, Nowgong, Sibsagar, Lakhimpur, parts of Naga Hills, and the district of Cachar (Barak valley) and Garo Hills (now in Meghalaya), including the adjacent Eastern Duars, which was under the Bhutanese influence in the early 19th century and was annexed by the British in 1866. On September 12, 1874 , the East Bengali district of Sylhet, historically unconnected to Assam, was included in Assam.

The primary goal of making Assam into a new administrative entity was to find an inexpensive and effective way to administer the area. Considerations of historical continuity or cultural contiguity were not in the minds of colonial officials. If one looks at racial, linguistic, and cultural affinities, the way to "lighten the burden of the Lieutenant Governor of Bengal" would have been to separate Koch Bihar from Bengal (Barpujari 1992, vol.4:275). But the Lieuterant Governor of Bengal, Sir George Campbell, was obsessed with the idea of the political boundaries of the new unit of Assam, coinciding with what he thought to be its natural boundary. The resultant decision to bring Sylhet into Assam "separated the Bengali-speaking people on either side of the Meghna, but engendered rivalry and antagonism between the two valleys of the Brahmaputra and Surma which continued with occasional breaks till our times" (*ibid*). A number of other territories annexed to the British Empire in subsequent years were incorporated into Assam, notably the country of the Lotha Nagas in 1875, that of the Angami Nagas in 1870-80, and of the Ao Nagas in 1889, and that of the Lushais (Mizo), conquered between 1871 and 1889 but constituted into a district of Assam in 1898. In a nutshell, colonial Assam, as an apparent from the

discussion so far, not only was larged than precolonical Assam; it excluded some areas that were culturally part of precolonial Assam.

Thus several aspects of the colonial political geography of Assam profoundly affected the subsequent cultural politics of Assam. Colonial political geography was part of what has been called Orientalism that evolved, paradoxically though but insidiously hard-in-glove with Aglicism, as a tool of colonial domination. Here it would suffice for our purposes if we focus on just two aspects of Assam's colonial geography: (i) the boundaries between the Nagas and the Assamese, and (ii) the notion of Asian as an extension of Bengal.

The Nagas and the Assamese: From Soft to Hard Boundaries

The course of Naga-Assamese relations is a good example of the constitutive effects of colonial geography on the politics of the region. The colonial rulers drew an internal boundary dividing the Nagas and the Assamese – an *Inner Line* – treating the Naga areas as an excluded area within Assam, almost similar on the lines of Manipur, severely restricting contact between Nagas and the Assamese as well as other Indians. The policy had its origin in practical considerations such as the establishment of clear and defensible property rights that were needed specially by the newly established tea plantations that were enchroaching on the land rights of the Nagas. The policy complemented the more ruthless military response of the British to attacks by "savages" on tea plantations" (Baruah 1999: 30).

There is ample evidence that in pre-colonial times the Nagas and the Assamese had substantive economic, cultural, and political relations. Folk tales speak of close, cordial relations. There is a story of a young Ahom King Godapani or **Lora Raja** (the boy King) fleeing and taking shelter among the Nagas. According to a legend, during the course of his stay in the Naga Hills, he married a Lotha Naga girl, then a Konyak, and then an Ao Naga girl. Later, as a sign of gratitude, the King granted some land to these tribes (Horam 1975:41). Naga claims to portions

of these lands were recognized until recently and plains villages paid taxes to the Nagas. This is a source of conflict between the Assamese and Naga villages even today and has indeed been termed "the very heart of the Assam-Nagaland boundary issue" (*ibid*: 6-7).

Historians agree that there were significant commercial and political ties between the Nagas and the Ahom Kingdom. There were land grants to Nagas in the plains, some Nagas fought in the Ahom armies, and Nagas sheltered Ahom princes fleeing from court conflicts. The Nagas close to the plains, whom the Assamese call **Bori** Nagas, acted as a batle between the Nagas of the interior (Abori) and the people of the valley. Verrier Elwin believed that the Ahom King considered the Nagas as "subjects and took taxes from them in the form of slaves, elephant tusks, spears, hand-woven cloth and cotton" (Elwin 1961:18). Edward Gait, the pioneering colonial historian of Assam, however, believed: that" the hilly tract inhabited by the various tribes known to us collectively as Nagas has never been subjected by the Ahoms" (Gait 1990:314).

It is not clear that Naga-Assamese relations can be framed in terms of the extremes of independence or subjugation. There is little doubt that the Nagas and the Assamese had substantial political, economic and cultural relations. For instance, the Nagas and the Ahom court had no understanding on the sharing of salt produced in the brine springs located in the Naga Hills. The Ahom Kings exercised ownership over a few of these springs. In other cases, Nagas manufactured salt and exchanged it with plainsmen for other goods. Perhaps the most powerful reminder of the historical connection is Nagamese that is alive and vital even today. Nagamese is a pidginized and subsequently creolized form of Assamese. The Nagas use it as a *lingua franca* among various Naga groups that speak different languages as well as in their interaction with the people from the plains.

The British colonial officials understood and made selective use of the ties between the Nagas and the Assamese for their own purposes. However, the selective appropriation of old institutions of inter-relationships in the early colonial period

gave way to a perception of a radical disconnection between the two communities. Overtime this became the new colonial common sense on the subject. There were ten "punitive expeditions" between 1875 and 1851 – bloody encounters when the colonial power as the vanguard of the "modern" responded to the resistance from the "primitive". This ultimately generated a mindset that became the foundation for a new policy that sought to segregate the hills from the plains, in this case the Nagas and the Assamese.

Assam as an Extension of Bengal

A second aspect of the colonial geography of Assam that has had long-term implications for the cultural politics of Assam was the notion that Assam is an extension of Bengal. This assumption, which had far-reaching implications, was justified by a British official in these terms: "Far from hindering national development, we are really giving it greater scope and enabling Bengal to absorb Assam" (A. Frazer, Note of December 6, 1904, cited in A. Guha 1977:71). From 1837 to 1873, Bengali was the language of the courts and government schools of Assam. While that was changed in 1873, the policy of encouraging large scale immigration from Bengal to Assam, as well as the way the boundaries of Assam were drawn, produced a demographic composition that kept Assam's language question a highly controversial one throughout the colonial period and beyond.

Early colonial administrators regarded the Assamese language as an offshoot of Bengali. The demand that Assamese be made the language of education out of the courts in Assam produced a major political controversy in the 1860s. Assamese public intellectuals argued that they were a distinctive people with a distinctive language and culture. They found an ally in an unexpected quarter – American Baptist missionaries who at that time were writing grammars and dictionaries of Assamese for their own reasons. Assamese intellectuals, in alliance with the missionaries, managed to convince British colonial officials of their case and Assamese became recognised as the language of Assam. This is how in short, the assertion of the autonomy and distinctiveness of Assamese language and culture became a central theme in the history of Assamese nationalism

In a nutshell, the cultural politics of an Assamese Assam and the resistance to being treated as a land frontier of Bengal became two central themes in the conflictual ethno-national politics of Assam. In post-colonial times starting with the formation of Nagaland in 1963, the hill areas were gradually separated from Assam, which was the culmination, in more than one way, of the colonial policy of segregation. Ironically, the creation of new states made the colonial assumption of a hard boundary between the hills and the plains somewhat of a reality. Much more ironically, one factor pushing the alienation of hills people from plains people was the Assamese desire to have cultural policies that defined the state as Assamese – a desire that was historically fueled by a politics of resistance to the other idiosyncracy of colonial geo-politics: the notion of Assam as an extension of Bengal.

The Present Context of Brahmaputra Valley

Present day Assam, particularly the Brahmaputra valley, has become a somewhat 'dangerous' place. There have been large-scale acts of political violence – kidnappings, murders, extortions, and ethnic violence. From time to time, gun-toting soldiers with specially endowed powers (e.g., the Armed Forces Special Powers Act (Assam and Manipur), 1958 and 1972) set up checkpoints to trackdown suspected militants. In rural areas, these soldiers go on regular expeditions in search of insurgents. In fact, the space for civic politics in Assam has greatly shrunk, yielding room to the politics of guns – wielded by insurgents, by the state, and often by "unknown assailants".

To an empathetic observer, it would be astonishing to see how quickly a 'democracy' can be totally reversed ethnic violence, politically forged violence by militant groups, state violence, and even violent crimes with a political subtext can all go on with impunity. It is all part of both the intended and unintended consequences of small decisions by various people, among them those vested with the authority of the Indian State. The vulgar display of the state's armed capacity has become a normal part of governance, co-existing with elections and the other rituals of democracy. As this has happened in Assam, the voice of

human rights activists has become faint in the din of national security ('unity and integrity', to add) talk among the pan-Indian Intelligentsia. Yet, pan-Indian ideas–laws, the constitution, and public discourse–have profoundly shaped these movements. The genesis of most of the conflicts has often been the result of misguided political practice by those acting with the authority of the state.

About two decades ago, both an outsider as well as an insider would identify an inhabitant of Brahmaputra valley (with "Assamese looks") as simply Assamese, in as much as they would do to identify a Bengali, a Gujarati or a Malayalee. In recent years, a new term, "ethnic Assamese" has come to be used, almost exclusively by the security forces and quite often in pan-Indian media and public discourse. In Assam's complex and political landscape, the category "ethnic Assamese" can define a category of people as a somewhat more likely target of suspicion, as a possible sympathizer and/or fellow traveller of the Assamese insurgents. The term "ethnic Assamese" typically characterises native inhabitants of the Brahmaputra valley, and as distinguishing Assam's many "immigrant" communities and the "tribal communities" – these, in recent decades, are less likely to be sympathisers of Assamese ethnic-national movement. The category, therefore, manages to distinguish, in terms of stereotypical phenotypes, a particular group of people in a way that seems to be related to the logic of surveillance and social control in Assam. Assam, as well as the Brahmaputra valley, within its boundaries, is a multiethnic place, and at the heart of many of the political and cultural conflicts is the fact that Assam is a land frontier with many "immigrant" communities. Since immigration, both during the precolonial and postcolonial periods, has been on of the crucial aspect of the Brahmaputra valley's multidimensional transformation, contributing substantively to the present day social tension and conflicts, movements and agitations, and even 'insurgency' and 'militancy', it is worthwhile to look at this phenomenon in some detail.

Assam remained a land frontier attracting large-scale immigration through much of the twentieth century. "Assam

has been the fastest growing area in the subcontinent for the past seventy years", wrote Ryron Weiner in 1978 (Weiner 1978:79). Indeed, Weiner, who was looking at Assam as a possible case study of migrant-local conflicts in India, soon discovered that it was a rather extreme and a typical case. Figures on immigrants in Assam, especially the Brahmaputra valley – the heartland of ethnic Assamese–have become a matter of intense political contestation, especially since the Assam movement of 1979-85. While the Assam movement itself focused on illegal immigration (and continues to do so even today), both supporters and opponents of the campaign relied on census data on population growth to make their case. Regrettably, census data are potentially explosive in today's Assam, almost similar to the entire north-east region.

The 1981 census could not be held in Assam because of the social and political unrest surrounding the Assam movement. Just prior to the 1991 census, there were many speculations on how Bengali speakers would identify themselves. There were some talks that Muslims of Bengali descent may not all choose to identify themselves as Assamese speakers as they had done in earlier census. That did not happen. The percentage of Assamese speaker in the 1991 population of 22.4 million decreased only slightly, from 60.9 percent of the total population in 1971 to 57.8 percent in 1991. Despite the politicization of the census, for purposes of at least crude approximation of the scale of immigration to Assam, there is no alternative to census data.

The Indian census collects data on place of birth and language that, under normal circumstances, should throw some light on Assam's immigration picture. These data, however, are utterly unreliable. The official in charge of the 1961 census observed that during emmumeration, in areas with abnormal increase, all persons gave as their birth place the place that they were living or a place that was within the same district, or, in some cases, another district in Assam. "As the birth place information of Assam in the 1961 census is completely unreliable," he warns, "the district-wise as well as the state immigration rate or the number of immigrants cannot be calculated even with the least degree of accuracy" (*Census of India 1961*: 71).

The census data on language are of not much help either. Indeed the census time series data on language in Assam make very interesting reading in terms of the sociology of official statistics. Apart from other things, the census in Assam has been a tool in the political management of tensions over immigration. Large number of immigrants – notably Muslims of Bengali language descent, but other communities as well – have been found to identify themselves as Assamese speakers, irrespective of whether they speak the language. As a result, Assam's census has some notable surprises. From 1911 to 1971, when Assam's population increased by 280 percent–from 3.8 million to 14.6 million – the proportion of Assamese speakers increased by 966 percent, from 21.69 percent to 60.89 percent of the population (Das 1989:44). The change of the percentage of Assamese speaker was a function of both changes in the scope of the territory called Assam and how certain groups of immigrants chose to identify themselves. It would be naive to assume that the change in the census self-definition always reflected adoption of the Assamese language.

Let us now try to very briefly describe the major immigrant communities of Assam, using certain ethnic categories. It is important to note however that the term "immigrant community" itself is problematical – even unfortunate – since perhaps only the first generation can be accurately described as immigrants. To refer to second/third generation offspring of migrants, who have adopted Assamese language and ways of living makes for a confounding irony. For instance, the Nepalis living in Assam and other parts of northeast India are part of a migration course from the hill areas of Nepal to a wider region that includes, besides northeast India, Sikkim, the Darjeeling region of North Bengal, and Bhutan. Yet, in the assertions of the rights of "indigenous peoples" vis-à-vis immigrants that have affected the entire region since the Assam movement, the Nepalis are not always seen as migrants. In Darjeeling they claim rights as indigenous people vis-à-vis Bengalis, and in Sikkim they are now the majority ethnic group and the major players in Sikkimese politics, their non-indigenousness being almost a non-issue most of the time (Rose 1999: 110-11).

The Tea Labour Community

The workers in the tea plantations constitute the oldest of Assam's large modern day "immigrant groups"; their recruitment from outside Assam began in the nineteenth century and continued until 1960. Most of these recruitees, mostly tribals from present day Bihar and Orissa, settled in Assam even after the contract period was over. While the 1921 census estimated the migrant workers and their descendants to be around 1.3 million (i.e. one sixth of the total population of the state at that time), by 1981 their number had increased to 3.4 million (Phukan 1984:123). Kar and Sharma observe that there are three different ethnolinguistic groups in Assam's tea garden labour community: (i) Kolarian speaking groups e.g. Munda, Santhal, and Kharia; (ii) Dravidian-speaking groups–Oraon, Kandh, Gond, and Malpahariya; and (iii) groups speaking Oriya, Bengali, and Hindi (1990:150). Yet, very few of the tea labour community today speak any of these languages; most of them speak a patois that is called *Sadani* or "Garden tongue" – often recorded in the census as Assamese. However, ethnic Assamese elite have accorded them low status, which has not always made it easy for them to become part of Assamese society.

Muslims of Bengali Descent

Given Assam's geographical location, the immigrants that colonial officials expected to come to Assam in large numbers were landless or land-poor peasants from East Bengal. Colonial officials saw land-abundant Assam as a solution to East Bengal's problem of land-scarcity. Their motivation was also partly political –balancing the Hindu and Muslim populations of Assam was undoubtedly an attractive tool of colonial political control. Though in the Census Report of 1881, Edward Gait expressed regret that economic forces alone were insufficient incentives for settlers from Bengal to come to Assam (cited in *Census of India* 1921:39), around two decades later the situation was completely different. The 1911 Census Report reported "the extraordinary in-course of settlers" to the "char lands" (islands of the river) of Goalpara, from the East Bengali districts of Mymensingh, Pabna, Bagra and Rangpur. Since then, the number of east Bengali immigrants,

mostly Muslims, went on increasing geometrically, so much so that by 1980s, it sparked off large scale anti-immigration politics in Assam.

With the partition of India in 1947, the continued migration from the area that became East Pakistan (and after 1971 Bangladesh) became a matter of crossing an international border. In the post-colonial period, economic immigrants were joined by an even larger group of political immigrants – Hindu refugees bearing Pakistan. During the War of 1971 that created Bangladesh, political refugees crossing into Assam included many Muslims.

Hindu Bengalis

Historically, the immigration of Hindu Bengalis – mostly for urban areas and to get jobs in the modern sector – has been a more persistent source of conflict in Assam than the Muslim peasant migration from East Pakistan. Unlike the Muslims of Bengali descent, Hindu Bengalis, especially those living in the Cachar district, are seen as active opponents of cultural politics that seek to give Assam a symbolically Assamese public face. However, Hindu Bengalis, especially those living in ethnic Assamese areas of the Brahmaputra valley, are no less inclined to speak Assamese and to participate actively in Assamese cultural life than the Muslims of Bengali descent.

The migration of Hindu Bengalis to Assam began in the early days of colonialising valley; colonialism as a new order required people with new skills – most obviously, command of the English language, to staff the new positions. Naturally, the people who came to staff the new positions in the colonial administration that were open to "natives" were mostly Bengali Hindus, who having been educated in colonial schools suited the positions. Besides their positions in the colonial bureaucracy, Bengali Hindus soon came to have a virtual monopoly in modern professions, e.g. medical, legal and teaching, apart from railways and the post office.

Protesting against the dominance of Bengali migrants in government offices and in middle-class occupations more generally was perhaps one of the earliest issues Assamese ethnic movement

took. Anandram Phukan complained that, even though a number of vernacular schools had been established, instruction in these schools was "imparted in a foreign language, viz. the Bengalese, which is but imperfectly understood by the teachers themselves, not to speak of the pupils" (Mills 1853: 205). In a way, Bengali was and continues to be considered more foreign than English in Assam, in as much as in Manipur.

The Marwaris

Another visible immigrant community in Assam is the "Marwaris", a term that is loosely used to refer to north-Indian ethnic groups, who along with the Rajasthan Marwaris, have been associated with trade and commerce in the region. Marwaris are quite likely to speak Assamese, especially since the trading ethos of the communities demands getting along with the locals. The Marwaris played a major role in introducing a moneytised economy into the erstwhile pre-monetised Assam. This was further accentuated by the tea labour community, and other immigrant workers working in coal and oil fields as well as peasants oriented to commercial agriculture. According to a 1906 government report, Marwari merchants "... monopolised practically the whole of the trade of the Assam (Brahmaputra) valley" (Allen 1960:75). As in other parts of India, Marwaris in Assam, in urban and rural areas and weekly hats, not only engaged in two way trading, i.e. selling products brought in from outside as well as collecting, at lower prices, local produces such as rice, pulses, jute or mustard and opium for export or reselling to the local populace at a higher premium, they also acted as moneylenders. The Marwaris of Assam are not a numerically large group, but their central role in the region's trade and commerce makes them highly visible. As Myron Weiner noticed:

> The Fancy Bazaar in Gauhati, perhaps the largest bazaar in northeastern India, is run predominantly by Marwari merchants. The Marwaris have their own charitable organizations, hospitals, Hindi-language newspapers and Hindi medium schools; they are thus not only economically better of than most Assamese, but their institutions and

> bazaars make them notably conspicuous and therefore vulnerable." (Weiner 1978:103-4).

While, by and large, there was no anti-Marwari violence until the 1960s, there have been mild expressions of resentment ever since the nineteenth century. In his petition to John Maffat Mills in 1852, Maniram Dewan complained of the "inhabitants of Marwars" as well as "Bengalees from Sylhet" being appointed as Mouzadars (Mills 1853:607). Some Marwari businesses have occasionally been targets of violence since the 1970s. During the Assam movement the rise of ULFA and the Bodo insurgency, Marwari businesses have been highly vulnerable to extortion demands by insurgents as well as other political organisations.

The Nepalis

Treaties between Nepal and India allow unrestricted travel of citizens (with some restrictions imposed in the second-half of 2000, as a result of the Kandhahar [Afghanistan] hijacking episode) between the two countries, along with rights to engage in economic occupations, to settle, and to own property. Another paradox about considering the Nepalese an "immigrant community" in Assam is that until 1980 Nepali cattle grazers were among the protected groups, along with the "Scheduled Tribes" in the areas known as "tribal blocks". There is still another paradox – relating to the category "Nepali". While in Nepal these "Nepali" emigrants actually are from "tribal" communities as well as from the Newari ethnic community in the Kathmandu Valley with separate ethnic identities, in northeast India they tend to identify themselves as a single Nepali or Gorkha community (Rose 1994:107). The 1991 census recorded 433,000 Nepali speakers, or 1.9 percent of the population. By and large, except perhaps during the Assam movement, anti-Nepali feelings in Assam have been rare.

We have listed only some of the major "immigrant communities"; there are other visible and sizeable "immigrant" groups as well. People from Bihar are engaged in some of the most arduous occupations in Assam as rickshaw drivers and in the construction of road, houses and buildings, as barbers and

cobblers. In recent years, however, they seem increasingly to be displaced by Muslims of Bengali descent in many of these occupations. There are migrants from Uttar Pradesh and Punjab engaged in trade and commerce along with the Marwaris. Indeed, many ethnic Assamese resent the fact that major commercial centers of Assam, notably Tinsukia, are by and large Hindi speaking places. The point of highlighting all this is to show how Assam got transformed from a low density to high density population, and from an overwhelmingly ethnic Assamese to a multi-ethnic, plurilingual society, mainly attributable to immigration during colonial rule. In fact, considering Assam's record of ethnic riots, political violence, insurgencies, human rights violations, and the slide towards a totally non-democratic polity – much of it rooted in the unresolved immigration tangle – one can try to appreciate the ethnic Assamese's perception of a threat to his/her identity, one of the most important symbol of which being language (Aggarwal 1994).

Cultural Politics of Language

The theme of asserting the autonomy and distinctiveness of Assamese language and culture, as virtually defining features of ethnic Assamese identity, is almost as old as the British conquest of Assam. British colonial officials in 1836, a decade after the takeover of Assam, had decided that the language of rule in Assam would be Bengali. The earliest assertions of Assamese cultural pride–well before it could be termed nationalism – grew as a reaction to that decision. As pointed out earlier, A.D. Phukan petitioned to Moffat Mills in 1852 against instruction in the "Vernacular Schools" being "imparted in a foreign language, that is, Bengali (Mills 1853:105). Thus the very first generation of modern Assamese intellectuals had to make the case that they were a distinct people with a distinct language and culture. Dhekiyal Phukan found an ally in American Baptist missionaries, who in the meantime were writing grammars and dictionaries. As a result of their efforts, in 1873 Assamese once again became the language of schools and of judicial proceedings. Assamese historical narratives of the nineteenth century typically refer to the period when Bengali was Assam's official language as a

"dark" period for Assamese language, literature, and culture.

In 1888, an organisation called Axomiya Bhaxa Unnati Xadhini Xobha (Association for the Development of the Assamese Language) was founded in Calcutta by Assamese students studying in what was called the capital city of colonial India. The establishment of this organisation is said to be "a landmark in the history of Assamese language and literature "(Barpujari and Sarma 1993:220). Among its most important projects was the standardisation of Assamese language. This concern with the question of "developing" the Assamese language deserves some comment.

The notion seemed to be that "developed" language is a sign of a "developed" people; so the "development" of the language could be the road to the "development" of the people speaking that language. Obviously, this formulation was shaped by the new ideas about modernity and progress, inherent in western, albeit English, education and knowledge. Lakhinath Bezbarua, one of the key figure of Assamese cultural, linguistic and literary nationalism, elaborates the curious connection that his generation made between the development of the Assamese language and the material progress of Assam. The goal of the Xobha, Bezbarua wrote, was to help the "tender mother tongue grow up to maturity", to enable the mother tongue to "reach the heights of other rich and prosperous languages of the world and illuminate with its glorious ways the face of .... poor and backward Assam" (cited in Neog 1976:3). The Axom Xohitya Xobha, in some way a success, or to the nineteenth century literary ferment had its first session in 1917. While we need not go into details of the Xobha's central role in the cultural politics of post-colonial Assam, suffice it to say that its fundamental motto was and is "my mother language-my eternal love".

In the three decades following India's independence in 1947, colonial Assam was divided into five states (Assam, Arunachal Pradesh, Meghalaya, Mizoram and Nagaland) and there are ongoing movements now for further division. The Assamese have come to see the break up of Assam as a mark of Assam's lack of control over its own destiny. The resultant

resistance to immigration and Assam's multiethnic landscape was not conducive to Assam becoming a language-based nation-province on the model of Bengal, Maharastra or Tamil Nadu etc. Further, the Bengali challenge to cultural policies that would define Assam as ethnic Assamese produced serious culture wars that even degenerated into "language riots".

The most notorious "language riots" in Assam were in 1960 and 1961, before and after the passing of the Official Language Bill by the State Assembly, "Riots" on a smaller scale occurred in 1972 over the decision of Gauhati University to switch to Assamese as the language of undergraduate education. In both instances, there were violent conflicts between ethnic Assamese and Hindu Bengalis resulting in deaths as well. Those killed became martyrs, and the deaths added to emotions that both sides could mobilize on the language question. For instance, one ethnic Assamese student, Ranjit Barpujari, who was killed by police firing during the language riots of 1960, is honoured as "the first martyr of the mother language". On the Bengali site, for instance, Paritosh Pal Choudhury's book *Cacharer Kanna* ('The Cry of Cachar') has a front piece with pictures of eleven garlanded dead bodies of people killed in 1961 as a result, again, of police firing on a demonstration in support of Bengali in Silchar" (Raychaudhary 1989:74-75).

The turmoil of 1960-61 ended with a compromise initiated by the Indian Congress leader, Lal Bahadur Shastri. He proposed that the Assam Official Languages Act be amended

a) to give local bodies the authority to alter the officials language of their area by a two-thirds majority;

b) to allow communication between the state capital and Cachar and the hill districts to continue to be in English;

c) at the state level to continue the use of English along with Assamese; and

d) to incorporate stronger provisions for the protection of linguistic minorities (*ibid*: 69-71)

Despite some opposition, the law was amended along these lines.

Another outbreak of "language riots" was in 1972, when Gauhati University decided to introduce Assamese as the language of education in the colleges under its jurisdiction. There was predictable opposition to this decision, especially from Bengali organisations. They wanted Bengali to be the language of college education not only in Cachar, but in the rest of Assam as well. After a tense period that included some outbreak of ethnic violence, the controversy came to an end, with the intervention of D.K. Barooah, then a member of Prime Minister Indira Gandhi's Cabinet. Barooah was an old hand in Assam politics. He suggested a compromise formula that allowed for the continuation of English and removed any compulsion on the matter of colleges switching to Assamese (Guha 1977:303). The most significant point to note here is that whenever ethnic conflict centered on the language question, it evolved heightened emotions and passions, leading to violence. And, in each case, the conflicts ended in a compromise – the compromise being the continuation of English, whether it was worked by Lal Bahadur Shastri, D.K. Barooah or someone else.

The English Language Teaching Contexts in North-East

In order to understand the sociolinguistic and ELT contexts in Assam and Manipur in a historical perspective, it is essential to glance at the colonial implantation and development of English in Assam and Manipur in some detail. While in the previous sections we have already examined the ethno-linguistic contexts in the Brahmaputra valley and the Imphal valley, including ethnolinguistic-Identity conflicts, here we will specifically focus on the origin, development and teaching of English in the two valleys.

English Education in the Brahmaputra Valley

During the British colonial period, the Assam scenario of education in general and English education in particular was not very different from that of India in a broad sense. But, there are significant differences as well. Since the history of English in Indian society, polity and education, in the colonial and post-colonial periods, is quite well-known in the literature on the

topic, we will not repeat it here. We will specifically focus on the differences.

Prior to the takeover of the Assam province (which then included five of the northeastern states) by the British, education, mostly religious and vocational in different arts and crafts, was restricted to the priestly and aristrocatic classes, scribes and a few other connected with the feudal rulers. After the province came under British colonial rule, the Assamese-language officers were found practically incompetent for tasks relating to colonial written documents, files, accounts etc. Hence, they were immediately in a phased manner, replaced by English-knowing babus from nearby Bengal (what is now West Bengal in India) who were well-versed in the art of colonial administration. While carrying out most of the written work relating to colonial administration in English for the benefit of colonial officials, these Bengali speaking officials, ironically, prevailed over the government to declare Bengali as the official language and the medium of education in the schools of Assam.

This drastic shift from Assamese to Bengali in the domains of education and administration attracted a large number of Bengalis to Assam on the one hand and rendered a great number of Assamese-speaking natives jobless. Captain Jenkins, the then Commissioner of Assam (1834-61), was alarmed by such a plight of the natives. In a pioneering effort, he took the first initiative to teach English to a large number of Assamese youth from urban centres in the Brahmaputra valley. Money, in the form of donation was collected for the purpose of establishing a school for the natives. Towards the end of 1835, with the approval of the General Committee on Public Instruction, an English-medium school was set up in Guwahati. Jenkins believed in the "Downward Filtration Theory", according to which education spreads gradually from the higher to the lower stratum of society. In case of time, the demand for English education grew so high that branch schools had to be set up at different places in Guwahati. This marked a remarkable beginning of English education in urban centers of Brahmaputra valley.

However, in the remote rural areas such schools fell far

short of popular demand. In order to cater to the needs of the village folk (in terms of English education, James Mathie, the then collector of Guwahati, worked out a scheme for setting up of village schools in August, 1938. This scheme prepared the establishment of Anglo-vernacular schools in the central locations of Brahmaputra valley (also known as Kamrup). In these schools, education was imparted both in English and the vernacular. In contrast, David Scott, the Agent to the Governor General of British India, has been reported to have set up eleven schools in Guwahati – schools in which the only language taught was Sanskrit. This was a clear example of the magical blend of Orientalism and Anglicism that scholars working in the area of colonial discourse have been talking about (see, for example, Aggarwal 1997 for a discussion of the Englit-English literature curriculum in India). Further, due to logistics and strategic reasons, large numbers of English-medium schools could not be set up. Hence, Jimes Mathie too supported the setting up of Sanskrit and Assamese medium schools so that the masses could be taught at least elementary reading and writing.

Quite expectedly, the minimal literacy that these Sanskrit and Assamese medium schools imported did not leap people in their search for better jobs or for upward mobility. Their job prospects remained restricted to semi-manual employment and lower rank jobs of clerks, copyists and the like. Too soon, people realized that to be materialistically better off and socially upwards mobile, they had to learn English. This made them demand for more and more English-medium schools. In mid-ninetieth century, only two full-fledged English-medium schools existed in the valley – one at Guwahati and the other at Sibsagar. The eagerness of the people to have English-medium education and the great demand for such schools became quite visible and evident, which was confirmed by the then Lieuterant Governor of Bengal, who wrote:

"There is a very strong desire on the part of all the better off classes of the community to give their children an English education, that wherever there was a school for teaching that language the attendance was good... Sudder stations where there

is none, people were clamouring for the establishment of one." (*cited in Barpujari* 1992:354).

This, in short and very broad terms, is the story of English gaining a firm ground in the Brahmaputra valley. It marked the beginnings of English education not only in urban centres like Guwahati and Sibsagar, it spread far and wide in rural areas as well. A little later, as the popularity and demand for English grew stronger, there emerged a demand for establishing a college that would mark the beginning of English higher education.

English in post-Independence Assam

As discussed above, English education was introduced in Assam by the British colonial rulers, but much later than in other parts of so-called mainstream India. It is important to note here that the term 'English education' is used here in a wider sense that includes the teaching of English language and literature as a subject as well as the use of English as a medium of instruction at different levels of education. In the beginning, by and large, the colonial officials accepted and encouraged the use of Assamese as the language of education, administration and judiciary. Assamese continued to be used in almost all departments of public office (for interaction with the natives) even after fifteen years of British occupation. But, in 1836, with pressure from Bengali 'babus' and patronage by a section of British officials, Bengali completely replaced Assamese in all domains of use in the public sphere. These Bengali officers enjoyed the patronage of the British since they were quite well-versed with the colonial system of administration. Additionally, they believed as well as convinced the British officers that Assamese was not an independent/separate language; that it was a dialect of Bengali, or rather a pervert version of Bengali. Consequent upon this, Mr. Robinson, then the Inspector of Schools in Assam province and Captain Jenkins, then the Commissioner of Assam, successfully persuaded the colonial government to declare Bengali as the Official Language of Assam. By hindsight, this dramatic shift from Assamese to Bengali in all public domains, including education and administration, was not all that smooth and linear. Quite sensitive and controversial was the question of the identity

of Assamese language – a distinctive language on its own or a pervert version/dialect of Bengali. This controversy on the question of linguistic identity continued to dog popular discourse in Assam during the period from 1836 to 1872. Yet, the dominance of Bengali over Assamese continued.

Predictably, such a conflicting sociolinguistic setting provided a fertile ground for English to flourish, quite like multilingual settings in India, Asia and Africa. English increasingly emerged as the most preferred language in the schools and colleges of Assam, both as a subject as well as the sole medium of instruction. This preference provided the fertile ground for the Christian missionaries to set up a large number of English medium schools all over the Brahmaputra Valley, of course with greater concentration in the tribal-dominated areas. The Assamese elite, on its part, developed a strong motivation for English education, since proficiency in English was then (as perhaps is now) the best guarantee of financial gain and upward mobility.

After Independence of India in 1947, controversies about the role and position of different languages, particularly English, Bengali and Assamese, in public domains raised their heads. The new social, cultural and political awakening that swept many parts of India because of engagement in the freedom of struggle and, paradoxically enough, because of exposure to western knowledge, ideas and concepts, affected the all-round context of Assam without exception. The unguarded spread of western (English) education, literature and philosophy gave rise to a new awakening in ethnic Assamese society as well. The strong preference for English education, resulting in the establishment of a large number of English-medium schools, entrenched the colonial language in ethnic Assamese society in the Brahmaputra Valley. Paradoxically enough, English gained a still firmer ground after the British left. And this trend continues even today.

However, a significant trend in the opposite direction has had emerged too. Many scholars, not very large in number though, took greater, active interest in indigenous philosophy, religion, culture, language, literature and the like. Systematic

study and research on different aspects of ethnic Assamese society followed. Linguistically, a negative attitude towards the continued higher (to Assamese) status of Bengali emerged, leading to, as pointed out in the earlier sections, ethnolinguistic conflicts, language riots and violence, resulting in loss of public life and property. All this made the sociolinguistic context of the Brahmaputra valley quite complex. We will discuss only a few aspects of this complexity, very briefly, in the following.

Assamese Language Movement and its Impact on the Sociolinguistic Setting

With the linguistic reorganisation of states following India's Independence, the regional languages and/or the 'majority' languages of the states were valorised by granting them the status of official languages. This in turn necessitated the introduction of these languages as media of instruction and administration in the respective states. First, in 1948-49, the *University Education Commission Report* (popularly known as the 'Radhakrishnan Report) and later, in 1964-66, the Education Commission Report (known as 'Kothari Commission Report) strongly recommended the use of regional languages (cf. ten confused with 'mother tongue') as medium of instruction at all levels of education, proceeding progressively from school to college to university levels Aggarwal 1988).

These changes in language policy and planning has had their impact in Assam as well which could not be an exception. In the early 1970s, the first step towards the regionalisation of medium of instruction was a resolution by Gauhati University to switch over to Assamese in all the colleges under its jurisdiction progressively from the academic session of 1972-73. However, due to language conflicts and language riots, a concession to use English as an alternative medium of instruction had to be made for colleges located outside the Brahmaputra valley. The strongest opposition to these provisions came from the Cachar District in the Barak Valley where people demanded the retention of Bengali as an alternative medium of instruction to Assamese. The Academic Council of Gauhati University which met on June 6,1972, in its attempt to contain the emerging conflicting

situation, decided to make two concessions for the linguistic minorities:

i) English was to be retained as the medium of instruction for a period of few years; and

ii) students were to be permitted to answer in the examinations in Assamese, English or Bengali.

The notification of these concessions immediately led to large scale protests and demonstrations in the Brahmaputra valley, demanding the withdrawal of the option of taking examinations in Bengali. Since, during the British rule, the Bengali-speaking officers and babus were the direct instruments of colonial exploitation, the negative sentiments and attitudes were stronger towards Bengali than English. Goswami records, "The Assam Sahitya Sabha backed up the position by passing a resolution to the effect that Assamese alone should be the medium of instruction in the Brahmaputra valley and English along with Assamese should be retained for a few years for answering in examinations (1997:71).

The Academic Council of Gauhati University was further forced to revise its decision of June 6 within just a week, i.e. on June 12, 1972. The revised resolutions read as follows:

i) Assamese shall be the medium of instruction in all colleges under the jurisdiction of Gauhati University.

ii) English shall continue as an alternative medium of instruction till such time, not exceeding ten years, as may be considered necessary by the Academic council.

iii) Students shall have the option to answer either in Assamese or in English in the University Examination.

iv) The above decision shall come into force with effect from the session 1972-73 in respect of two-year pre-University course and from the session 1974-75 in respect of two year degree course. (quoted in Goswami 1997:72)

Subsequently, on September 23,1972, the Assam Legislative Assembly resolved that the medium of instruction for both the

Gauhati University and the Dibrugarh University at the university stage would be Assamese, but English was also to remain as a medium of instruction.

The language conflict did not end there. Far from it, students from the Brahmaputra valley, led by the All Assam Students Union (AASU), strongly opposed this resolution of the State Assembly on the grounds that (i) it had failed to accord due status and recognition to Assamese language, and (ii) the resolution would convert Assam into a bilingual state. The AASU, backed by the Assam Sahitya Sabha, turned its opposition to a powerful movement, which sporadically snowballed into civic violence. Ultimately, the Assembly had to decide to withdraw its September,1972 Resolution and to honour the Gauhati University Resolution.

According to the new decision, Assamese was to be made the sole medium of instruction in the Brahmaputra valley, while Assamese would be taught as a subject in non-Assamese and linguistic minority schools. The virtually euphoric assertion in favour of Assamese issued from a sense of insecurity that resulted from the century old dominance of the Bengali language on the former. Goswami aptly remarks, "As language in this country stood for and represented culture, race, history, individuals and finally a sub-nation (1997:7), the people of Assam had valid reasons for exercising their language rights. While the integrative and symbolic functions were performed by this valorisation of Assamese, the switch over from English and Bengali to Assamese in education did not receive any great boost and its implementation proved to be difficult. In fact, the latest statement on language in education, contained in the National Policy on Education-1986 concedes, for the first time, officially that throughout India the switch over from English to the mother tongue(s) of the learner had failed. The 1986 document recommended vigorous efforts at implementation towards the stated policy. There remains, however, a great hiatus between the stated policy and practice in reality. In all kinds of institutions of higher education, English continues to have its monopoly. Last, one does not have to carry out any great research to observe the mushrooming of English

medium schools, the great demand for 'standard' English education, and the increasing use of English not only in public domain but in private domains as well during the past one decade, apparently due to the liberalisation and globalisation of Indian economy. Assam clearly has not (and, perhaps cannot) insulate itself from the great impact of these forces.

It has already been pointed out that in the late nineteenth and early twentieth centuries, Bengali had increasingly made inroads into Assam's society and polity. A different wave, which is of prime importance for the present study, however, in favour of English Education, had swept over the province, especially among the Assamese elite inhabiting the urban centers. Important documents such as the letters in *The Orunodoi* (Neog 1983) provide us with meaningful glimspes of the powerful hold of English on the Assamese society:

FIRST LETTER TO THE LITTLE READERS OF ORUNODOI

(Orunodoi porha saru lorabilakar pratiprothom pranaya potra)

> "... Till 1800 years ago, the English people wore only animal skins and they used to eat even flesh of animals. But now they are the most wealthy and intelligent people of this world. If you want to know how it has become possible, you will have to go through the English literature and that is why you will have to know the language. But, it is not possible for all to learn English and read their literature; so those who can learn the language should learn it and then they should translate the English literature into Assamese...." [September 1946, Vol.2, No.9].

SIXTH LETTER FROM CALCUTTA

(Kalikotar pora sostha patra)

> "...It is wisdom and knowledge which makes the difference between man and animals. And in order to spread knowledge many schools are established in the British occupied Assam, but since they use 'foreign language textbook', it is of no use to our boys. Priests use Assamese textbooks in their Missionary Schools but the fact is that most of the boys do not go to such schools because of the fear that they might be converted into Christians..."[April 1854, Vol.IX, No. 7].

It is clear that in the beginning there were strong objections, especially from feudal, brahmanical and aristocratic families, to give English education to their wards. For example, the famous Assamese lexicographer and writer, Hem Chandra Barooah (1835-1895) had to secretly teach English, without the consent or even knowledge of his parents, who were orthodox Brahmins. Paradoxically, but not surprisingly, when his guardians learnt that proficiency in English enabled Hem Chandra get a government job, he was encouraged to continue his pursuit. Hence, though, the spread of English education in Assam, more particularly in the Brahmaputra valley, had to face a variety of obstacles in the initial stage, these obstacles were overcome to a large extent, clearly due to instrumental motivation.

Interestingly, the British officers themselves realised the impossibility and, most importantly, the dangers of completely replacing Assamese by English in public domains. Francis Jenkins, the then Commissioner of Assam (1834-61), considered it essential to win over the feudal aristocracy who had lost their power and influence on British occupation and for whom, he thought, the government must provide employment. To this end, he brought home to the government of India, in his letter of June 21, 1834:

> "These few [Assamese] in their present uneducated stage do not suffice to carry on the duties of our courts, the office in which are mostly filled by natives of Sylhet and Rangpoor. So that the old families of Assam are still there in their own native province from being elbowed [out from] those situations which lead to power or decent maintenance. This state of things appears to be pregnant with evil and I know no other method by which it could be remedied than by the government taking some active measures to provide instruction for the Assamese youth." (Quoted in Barpujari 1992, Vol.IV: 349)

This brief quote unambiguously indicates that Jenkins intuitively understood that to continue British colonial rule in Assam, it was essential to make the traditional aristocracy its close ally and that language proficiency was directly related to power, influence and economic well-being. He strongly urged the government to import English education, under the supervision

of local authorities, at Sadar Stations: Goolpara, Guwahati, Nagaon, Darang and Biswanath. To achieve the objectives sooner than later, willing young persons of rank were to be sent to Calcutta and provisionally teachers competent in teaching English and Bengali had to be brought in from Bengal.

True to the expectations of Jenkins, when the portals of public services were thrown open to those natives who have had 'some' English education, the higher classes not only clamoured for English education for their sons (daughters then were not to be given formal education), many of them became patrons of such education. The increasing demand for English education led to the opening up of a number of what were called 'branch' schools, entirely at public expense, in the neighborhood of Guwahati – Pandu, Kamakhya, Beltola, Amingaon and North Guwahati. Due to pervasive poverty and ignorance, people in rural areas were "content to live and die as their forefathers did". Yet, many desired at least rudimentary educational opportunities to be available nearer home. The demand for education, which then meant almost exclusively English education, became all the stronger with the introduction of new (colonial) revenue laws and measures in 1833-34, requiring the services of good number of lower rank revenue officers such as the "thakurias" and "gaon kakaties" etc. The introduction of written pattas (land records) not only created great confusion and curiosity, but it necessitated a minimal knowledge of the 3-Rs to guard one's (landed) property and oneself from being deceived and cheated out by corrupt **omlahs** of the courts. Evidently, on the whole, English education successfully spread its tentacles in Assam primarily due to two reasons: (I) the lure of government jobs of different ranks; and (ii) the fundamental need to protect one's land.

The position of English did not change much in the post-independent India or Assam. The "uncomfortable compromise" (Aggarwal 1988) that was reached through the Constituent Assembly Debates, the language provisions in the Constitution of India and the Official Language Act, 1963, virtually perpetuated the important role of English in public domains. The situation

in Assam has not been very different, except for the fact that, as pointed out earlier, the hostility towards Bengali language was much greater than that against English.

To reiterate, there has been a considerable increase in the number of schools, high schools and colleges in the post independent era in Assam. Prior to 1962, secondary education in the state was dually controlled by the Gauhati University and the Department of Education. In 1972, the Board of Secondary Education of Assam (SEBA) was created and it took over the responsibility of looking after the academic aspects of the schools. With regard to medium of instruction, though the state government had accepted the recommendations of the Education Commission, 1964-66 and its concommitant Three Language Formula (cf. Aggarwal 1988) which the SEBA was to operationalise, regionalisation of the medium of instruction could not be affected. Due to strong protests against making Assamese the sole medium of instruction, along with other Indian languages like Bengali, Hindi, and a couple of minority, tribal languages, English continued to be used as a medium of instruction in many educational institutions. In recent decades, and particularly after the liberalisation of the economy, the number of students learning English and the demand for English-medium schools in Assam have been multiplying. Not surprisingly, recently, in 1998, the government of Assam has decided to introduce English at the primary stage of education, even in the regional medium schools.

To explain this paradox by saying that English continue to command great respect and demand and the popular support for one's mother tongue, in this case Assamese, is merely a question of political opportunism or hypocritical middle-class elitism would be only partial and too simplistic. Undoubtedly, large sections of people support their mother tongue, viz. Assamese in the Brahmaputra valley for various concerns such as ethnic identity, survival of the language, native culture and literature. Superficially, it may appear to some that these people are more concerned with the existence of the language rather than the growth and development of the language. This may be partly true, but the issue is far too complex and beyond the scope of this study.

What is of greater interest is the ambivalent attitude the ethnic Assamese people have towards bilingualism. Borah (1998:50), by referring to Philipson (1992) thinks that, like western societies, people in Assam as well associate bi-multilingualism with poverty, powerlessness and the like. Borah (ibid) further elabourates on the impact of the monolingual ethos of British ELT in Assam. These are serious questions that demand greater theoretical reflection and empirical exploration to make any meaningful advance. We would return to these issues when we examine our empirical data.

English Education in Manipur

Neither the history nor the development and the contemporary context of English education in Manipur have been as well documented as in the case of Brahmaputra Valley. However, by tracing the fragments that we were able to locate from different sources, we may attempt a broad outline of the history and development of English education in Manipur.

A British Political Agency was established in Manipur in 1836. The following year in 1837, Captain Gordon, the first Political Agent of Manipur, sowed the seeds of English education in the Manipur principality, and that too at his own expense. However, due to a variety of cultural, social, financial and economic factors, Gordon's project of English education was short-lived. About 35 years later, in 1872, Major General W. H. Nuthall, the then Political Agent, opened a school at Imphal, with English as the medium of interaction. However, it was his successor, Sir James Johnstone (1876-86), who laid the foundation of English education in the Manipur valley, despite a number of obstacles. Sir Johnstone prevailed upon the Maharaja of Manipur to open an English School, which was established and named after the former in 1885.

Initially, the School was run within the premises of the British Residency Compound (presently the Raj Bhavan of Manipur State) as a private school. Following the Anglo-Manipuri War in 1891, the school had to be closed down. Almost a year later, on June 1, 1892, the school was reopened, but, for 'security

reasons', it was relocated outside the Residency Compound. From this time onwards, the number of students enrolment went up steadily. A pucca building for the exclusive use of the school was built in 1893. The school started with a bang with 117 students on its rolls (Aruna Devi 1990). Now, the School, renamed as Johnstone Higher Secondary School, is the pride of Manipur, imparting education from the primary level to the higher secondary level. Thus began the spread of English education in the valley of Manipur.

The story of the spread of English education in Manipur would remain pathetically incomplete without recording the contribution of Rev. William Pettigrew. Rev. Pettigrew, a Christian missionary as well as a scholar – educationist par excellence, came to Manipur on February 6, 1893 (*ibid*: 11). Because of objections from the Maharaja of Manipur, the Manipuri brahmanical order and the aristocracy, Pettigrew was not allowed to carry out missionary work in the valley. Left with no choice, Rev. Pettigrew undertook and concentrated on the task of consolidating and supervising the spread of education in the valley. He started a number of schools, viz. Thangmeiband L.P. School and Tera Keitheil U.P. School, among others. While waiting at Silchar (Cachar district of Assam) for his 'entry permit' to Manipur, Pettigrew had mastered Manipuri language with the help of some Manipuri inhabitants of Silchar. With this knowledge of the language, he performed the pioneering task of producing the first ever *Manipuri Primer, Manipuri Grammar* and a number of textbooks, and the outstanding *English-Bengali-Manipuri Dictionary*.

Since Rev. Pettigrew had to face a number of serious obstacles and troubles because of his (religious) missionary zeal, he had to leave for Ukhrul, a prominent and exclusive habitation of Tangkhul Naga tribe on high hills, where he could freely carry out both his missionary work and educational projects. In January 1896, Rev. Pettigrew left the Valley to settle down at Phungyo village near Ukhrul for good. Since the topic of English education in the hills of Manipur is beyond the scope of this study, we will not discuss it any more.

In spite of Pettigrew's departure, English education had gained very strong ground in the Valley and by 1896, i.e. within a span of just five years, there was remarkable growth in the valley. By 1890, there were 2 middle class and 56 lower primary schools in the Valley, with 221 boys and 6 girls and 3380 boys and 11 girls enrolled in them respectively (Joychandra 1988:37). By 1920, there was still greater growth in the number of students enrolled. The following table provides the comparative figures showing a decadal growth between 1910 to 1920.

Decadal Growth of Education in the Valley of Manipur

Year	*No. of Schools*	*Type of School*	*No. of students*	*Enrolled*
			Boys	*Girls*
1910	2	Middle English	221	6
	56	Lower Primary	3380	11
1920	2	Middle English	257	0
	3	Upper Primary	255	0
	72	Lower Primary	5527	24

Source: Joychandra, N.(ed.) 1988. *Freedom Forty: Pragatontra Supplement. Imphal,* August 15, 1988; P.37.

The year 1907 was also significant in the history of English education in Manipur, for quite a different reason, viz. the Johnstone High School was granted affiliation upto Class X by Calcutta University. In 1929 – 30, the Calcutta University opened a Matriculation Examination centre in Imphal, located at the Johnstone High School. From then on, English (as well as Manipur) education has never looked back – from a paltry 17 Government schools in 1920, the number of such schools had increased to 2934 by 1990 and, according to a rough estimate, it has gone up to about 3300 at the turn of the century. It is important to point out that most of this growth, quantitively speaking, has occurred after the Britishers left.

English continues to occupy an important place in education

in post- Independent Manipur. Here, in the Government Schools, set up and fully funded by the State Government, the regional language – Manipuri – Meiteilon is the sole medium of instruction, but English as a second language is introduced as early as in Class II. The Board of Secondary Education Manipur (BSE) Impahl; the Council of Higher Secondary Education, Imphal and the State Council for Educational Research and Training (SCERT), Imphal together produce textbooks for these schools as well as conduct workshops, refresher courses and other in-service teacher-training programs for teachers of English in the state.

In Manipur, English enjoys an overwhelmingly high status and does not suffer from even the mildest kind of opposition. Further, Manipuri (or Meiteilon) is the Official Language of the State of Manipur. Quite unlike the case of Assam, Manipuri does not come into conflict with any dominant language, though during the movement for the inclusion of Manipuri language in the Eight Schedule of the Constitution of India, there were anti-Hindi feelings, slogans and protests, because Hindi represented the unresponsive Central Government. Anti - Hindi feelings also exist even now because of the large scale human rights violations by the Hindi-speaking security forces of the Indian state. However, Manipuri and English exist in near perfect peaceful co-existence in the state.

Though Manipuri is the Official Language of the state, in practice most work in courts, administration, and all kinds of state and district level public offices as well as in urban, elite private establishments, is conducted in English. English is the sole medium of instruction in all institutions of higher education, including general education, colleges, polytechnics, Science & Technology institutions, Manipur University and the Central Agricultural University, while English is taught as a subject in Government and Govt.–aided schools, missionary and non-missionary English medium schools far out-number Manipuri medium schools and there is still demand for more such schools. In many English medium schools, use of any other language other than English within the school premises invites physical

punishment and financial penalty. Clearly, the wallet – value of the language and the Manipuri – Tribal competition in the field of education and employment, making learning of English the most valued one. Apart from enjoying high social prestige, a strongly favourable attitude, proficiency in English marks one as 'educated'. In other words, only one who knows English well is treated as a 'learned' person.

3

THE EMPIRICAL STUDY

The empirical study was carried out in order to explore the ground reality and see whether the findings of such a study match, partially match or do not match at all with the theoretical formulations, hypotheses and propositions discussed in Chapter – 1. The empirical survey was carried out additionally to examine and correlate the findings of the study from a multi-dimensional perspective, keeping in mind the quite elaborate review of the literature on the two ethnolinguistic communities (the ethnic Assamese and the ethnic Meeteis) presented in Chapter – 2.

Objective of the Study

As already stated in the Introduction, the overall objective of the study is to examine critically the being and becoming of the power and politics of English in North-East India from a socio-pedagogic point of view. However, in view of our specific focus in the study, planning, designing and executing the study and, of course, limitations of time and space, we have had to make minor changes in programmatising the empirical study. While most sociolinguistic studies in the country, by and large, focus on the formal linguistic aspects following the Labovian/ the functionalist approaches, they have put the "socio" component only as a token backgrounder. In the present study, we consider it as of greater significance not simply to focus but to deal in an elaborate way with the historical, sociological, anthropological, political and related aspects of the people we chose to study. Hence, there is virtually no formal linguistic data presented in the study. Furthermore, it is an apparent weakness of the study as presented here that the pedagogic aspect has not received the

attention it deserves and as it was attempted to be dealt with. As we proceeded with the study, we found it really difficult to balance the 'socio' and 'pedagogic' aspects. We had no choice left but to go with greater emphasis on the 'socio' component of it, clearly at some cost of the pedagogic aspect. Since, virtually no study of English in the North-East exists, it was our considered decision to approach the problematic from what Fasold (1984) would call the 'Sociolinguistics of society'. In a nutshell, the present study should hopefully provide the basis for future research on the problematic which could focus on micro-perspectives within the broad spectrum of applied-sociolinguistics of English in the North-East India.

The specific objectives of the study, as they emerged, developed, got systematised and finally, were worked out, may be listed as follows:

(a) to gather information on the socio-economic background of the respondents from the two ethnolinguistic communities. This was meant to provide us with the comparative profiles of the English-speaking upper-middle-class elite of the two communities;

(b) to find out the respondents' use of English in different domains, particularly within the broad framework of the field, mode and tenor of discourse;

(c) to gather information on the multilingual repertoire of the people and the reported use to which such a repertoire was subjected;

(d) to find out and examine people's preferences for, attitudes towards and loyalty to the various languages in the context of individual and societal multilingualism;

(e) to decipher, indirectly, the people's individual and collective perceptions regarding the power and politics of English in their respective communities; and

(f) to see if the inferred and examined understanding and perception of the people could fit into language policy decisions and language planning.

Methodology

Even though, on the surface, it may appear that we have adopted the typical questionnaire survey methodology, our approach indeed has been of a completely different sort. We adopted an entirely flexible and informal methodology for the study. With our own understanding of the macro contexts in Assam and Manipur, we carried on lengthy formal and informal discussions with different people at different levels. Simultaneously we kept on looking for any published or memeo material that could be relevant to the present study. In the process, we found very little published material on the sociolinguistic problematic as a whole, and, literally, none at all on the question of English. Frustrating though this experience was, it led us to a vast treasure of historical, sociological and anthropological literature, most of which contained references to language issues as part of the overall existential problems of the communities in the region.

Clearly, our own starting point that linguistic issues could not be separated from the overall social context was more than vindicated. Ranging from questions of ethnic and racial origins to the contemporary controversies relating to education and employment, everywhere the language problematic was enmeshed with the variety of non-linguistic dimensions. This realisation guided us throughout the work. Hence, even though we had a structured and cyclostyled questionnaire as a reference point, in the process of gathering information on individuals, societies and communities, their multi-dimensional features of linguistic being and becoming and analysing all these information for our study, we collated everything together, rather than isolating linguistic issues. And, this formed the basic methodology for the present work.

Sampling

Sampling was done in a completely random and intuitive way. As a native of Manipur and a teacher of English in Assam, the researcher used his own intuitive understanding of what would constitute a representative sample for the present study. A couple of points need to be noted here. Firstly, no available

sampling procedure was followed. Given the virtually round the year law and order problems and the concurrent inaccessibility to areas, localities and to individuals (due to massive presence of security forces as well as private armed groups), we have had no choice but to proceed as the situation led us to. Secondly, as a corollary to the foregoing, sampling became an ongoing process throughout the study. As we took stock of the progress in the empirical study, we did identify major gaps in the sampling which we tried to bridge by going to the fields with the major gaps in mind. But we have had to put a stop to the empirical study at some point. With our own understanding of what could be a representative sample of the English-speaking elite in the region, we had to conclude our field survey. The details of the respondents so chosen have been given in Chapter – 4.

Questionnaire Survey

Quite a detailed questionnaire was designed containing three major sections and twenty six major questions, some of which were open-ended while others were restricted to certain given choices. We had to keep in view the difficulties of analysing a completely open-ended questionnaire, which, of course, we prefered for the kind of study we have undertaken.

The questions in the questionnaire related to the following:

(i) socioeconomic profile of the respondents;

(ii) multilingual repertoire;

(iii) self-reported proficiency and language use of different languages in different domains for different purposes;

(iv) language preferences;

(v) language attitudes;

(vi) loyalty to language; and

(vii) lastly, the implicit perceptions of the role, status and position of English in its various extra-linguistic dimensions.

The questionnaire, so worked out and implemented is presented as an Appendix. The different questions and sub-

questions have also been discussed in detail in Chapter – 4.

Diary Notes

The researcher maintained very roughly drafted notes as diary notes throughout the period of the field survey. These notes included the different kinds of problems and difficulties encountered by the researcher, in terms of approaching various locations and personalities which range from high ranking bureaucrats and police officials on the one hand and ground level social activists on the other. The researcher also made diary notes of the problems faced by respondents in terms of responding to a structured questionnaire as well as hesitations, confusion, lack of interest and clarity on the part of the respondents. All of these have been combined and made use of in the analysis of the field survey data in Chapter-4. The diary notes have run into about 20 pages. Since the major points from the diary notes have been included in the analysis, we decided not to put them in the Appendix. An important component of the diary notes is the emotional reaction of the researcher in terms of feelings of relaxation as well as sense of failure.

Comparing: Manipur and Assam

Given the enormity of the people's multidimensional diversity, we have had to isolate two relatively least diverse communities – the ethnic Assamese Hindus in the Brahmaputra Valley and the Hindu Meeteis in the Manipur Valley. Propositionally, as the two ethnic-linguistic communities form more relational societies in popular perceptions, our guiding principle was comparative, i.e. to look into similarities as well as differences. These similarities and differences were to be identified and examined not simply in inter-ethnic terms but also in terms of intra-ethnic group differences. For example, what could be assumed as a relatively homogenous and undifferentiated community was found to be both horizontally and vertically stratified. The same holds equally true for the ethnic Assamese society. It is precisely because of this that we chose to present and analyse both secondary information as well as primary data within a broad comparative paradigm.

4

THE FIELD SURVEY

Socioeconomic Background

Table 1 (A and B) presents information on the socioeconomic background of the respondents. While Table 1A represents the combined figures of Assam and Manipur, Table 1B makes a comparative statement. We wanted to see if there were any remarkable differences in terms of socioeconomic variables between the respondents from Assam and Manipur and whether these differences have any significant bearing on the responses to our questions on language proficiency, language use and language attitudes.

As can be seen from Table 1A, a great majority of our respondents (sample) belong to the active lower and higher middle age groups. We have 43 (19.0%) respondents belonging to the age group 10-25, representing the younger generation of students or very fresh recruits into jobs. In the age group 26-40, we have 97 (42.9%) respondents representing the highest figure who we have broadly called the 'middle' age group, and who represent that section of educated people in society who have entered and have had some experience of gainful employment. We have called the age-group 41-55, 67(29.6%) of the total respondents, as 'higher middle age' since this is the group representing people who have been in their occupations for a decade or more and whose perceptions, attitudes and reactions can be taken as virtually unchangeable. In the age-group 56 + we have 19(8.4%) respondents and they can be taken as either outdated, outgoing or as the determining force depending on the nature of the society, i.e. in terms of the ascribed and/or expected roles of different age groups.

In terms of 'sex', we have 135 (59.7%) males and 91 (40.2%) females out of a total of 226. Though our age and sex representations is not strictly statistically or demographically representative, they can be taken as the most appropriate samples for looking at English sociolinguistically. We will comment on this later in the discussion.

Next, with regard, to educational qualifications we have 53(23.4%) respondents 'below graduation', meaning thereby that these respondents had different levels of schooling and collegiate education but have not acquired any degree as such. This is the category, which in a comparative sense would be expected to have the lowest proficiency in English and therefore a completely different use of an attitudes towards the language from the rest of the sample. There are 67 (29.6%) 'Graduates' (B.A., B.Sc. and B.Com. etc.) and 73 (32.3%) 'Post–graduates' (M.A, M.Sc., M.Com., M.Phil., Ph.D. etc.) The rest 33 (14.6%) of the respondents have had what is known as and/or professional / vocational education leading to award of degrees or diplomas such as B.E., B.Tech., LL.B., LL.M., M.B.B.S.,M.S., M.D., B.V.Sc., ... In a way, we had selected respondents who were expected to have had at least the minimal educational experience so as to have some kind of meaningful relationship with English and those whose very professional life depended to a lesser or greater extent on their mastery of English.

Occupationally, we have 39 (17.2%) 'students'; 32 (14%) 'teachers'; 23 (10.1%) 'professionals'; 15 (6.6%) 'media personnel'; 11 (4.8%) 'security personnel'; 9 (4.0%) 'general administrators'; 10 (4.4%) 'educational administrations'; 16 (7.0%) 'private sector employees'; 33(14.6%) 'public sector employees'; 11 (4.8%) 'performing artists'; 3(1.3%) 'creative artists'; 10(4.4%) 'NGO volunteers'; 14(6.1%) 'others'. Now, some clarification on these somewhat adhoc categorisation of occupational groups is in order here. The category 'students' cannot be strictly taken as an occupational category and yet we have the highest representation of 'students' in our sample. This is because we thought the students in any society reflected the future in terms of English as well as all other aspects. The category 'teachers'

includes those who are in the teaching profession from the school level to the university level. In fact in this category we have included a few but the most influential (senior) Professors of English and other subjects. The other categories represent the respondents' 'occupation' as below:

Professionals	:	doctors, engineers, lawyers etc.
Media Personel	:	reporters and journalists in the print media as well as other associated with the electronic media
Security Personnel	:	police, paramilitary and army personnel ranking from jawans/constables to D.G.P./ Brigadier (Colonel) in the police, para-military and military forces
General Administrators	:	civil officials of high rank.
Educational Administrators	:	principals, directors of education, deputy registrar of University etc.
Private Sector	:	business people ranging from small traders to big – bulls, travel agents, automobile dealers etc.
Public Sector	:	ranging from grade IV employees to Class II officers in various Govt. and semi–govt. departments.
Performing Artists	:	actors, actresses, film makers, theatre workers etc
Creative Artist	:	writers and critics
NGOs	:	volunteers and organisers of different NGOs engaged in health, enviroment, AIDS, cultural and social activists
Others	:	politicians, sports personalities, house wives etc.

In terms of place of 'birth' and 'residence' we have had a fairly representative distribution between urban, semi-urban

and rural, places. While 61(26.97%) were born in urban areas, 83(36-71%) and 82(36.2%) of the respondents were born in semi-urban and rural places respectively. In terms of residence, that is, the present place where the person lives and works, 87 (38.4%), 80(35.3%), 59(26.1%) of our respondents reported as residing in urban, semi-urban and rural places respectively. The only significant observation we can make here is the characteristics migration of people born in rural places but working in urban places.

In terms of 'income' we have 6(2.6%) respondents whose income is below Rs.1,000/- and 45(19.9%) persons who have not indicated their income at all. Presumably most of these respondents are students who have no income of their own or persons working in NGOs and other related fields without any income worth mentioning. In fact about 50 percent of the sample, that is 83(36.7%) and 29(12.8%) have income ranging from Rs.5,001 – Rs. 10,000 + respectively. Perhaps, this is the group that is conventionally called the educated middleclass English speaking elite.

In terms of religion we took care to have a more undifferentiated sample for simplicity of analysis. So we have 201(88.9%) a vast majority of Hindus and the rest 25(11.0%) belong to smaller categories including Buddhists, atheists and revivalist of pre-Hindu religions etc.

Table 1 B provides the comparative socio-economic profile of the respondents from Assam and Manipur, As we see from this Table, there are minor variations between the two states in almost in terms of all the variables, but the differences are not so significant so as to require any special interpretation. What, however, needs special comment is in terms of place of residence and birth and the categories of 'urban', 'semi-urban' and 'rural'. In the context of Assam, the distinctions between urban, semi-urban and rural are comparatively more clear-cut and non-controversial. Guwahati as a capital city is clearly urban, smaller towns in the inner districts and sub-divisions can be clearly identified as semi-urban and rural. But, in the context of Manipur, the capital city of Imphal itself presents some problems of categorisation. While Imphal downtown can be considered as

Table 1A
Socioeconomic Background

Age		*1-25*	*26-40*	*41-55*	*56 +*	*Total*	
		47 (19.0%)	97 (42.9%)	67 (29.8%)	19 (8.4%)	226 (100)	
Sex			Male 135 (59.7%)	Female 91 (40.2%)	Total 226 (100)		
Eductional Qualifications		*Below graduates*	*Graduates*	*Post Graduates*	*Professional Graduates & Vocational Diploma Holders*	*Total*	
		53 (23.4%)	67 (29.6%)	73 (32.3%)	33 (14.6%)	226 (100%)	
Occupation	*Students*	*Teachers*	*Professionals*	*Media Personal*	*Security Personal*	*General Admini-strators*	*Educational Admini-strators*
	39 (17.2%)	32 (14.1%)	23 (10.1%)	15 (6.6%)	11 (4.8%)	9 (4.0%)	10 (100%)

	Pvt. Sector Employees	Public sector Employees	Performing Artists	Creative Artists	NGO Volunteers	Others	Total
	16 (7.0%)	33 (14.6%)	11 (4.8%)	3 (1.3%)	10 (4.4%)	14 (6.1%0	226 (100%)
Residents		*Urban*	*Semi Urban*	*Rural*	*Total*		
		87 ((38.4%)	80 (35.3%)	59 (26.1%)	226 (100%)		
Place of Birth		61 (26.9%)	83 (367%)	82 (36.2%)	100%		
Income	*Below Rs. 1000*	*Rs 1001-5000*	*Rs. 5001-10000*	*(Rs. 10000 +*	*No Response*	*Total*	
	6 (2.6%)	63 (27.8%)	83 (36,7%)	29 (12,8%)	45 (19.9%)	226 (100%)	
Religions		*Hindu*	*Others*	*Total*			
		201 (88.9%)	25 (11.0%)	226 (100%)			

Table 1B
Socioeconomic Background

	Assam	Manipur	Assam	Manipur	Assam	Manipur	Assam	Manipur	Assam	Manipur	Assam	Manipur	Assam	Manipur
Age			*10-25*		*26-40*		*41-55*		*56+*		*Total*			
			26 (21.8%)	17 (15.8%)	49 (41.1%)	48 (44.8%)	36 (30.2%)	31 (28.2%)	8 (6.7%)	11 (10.2%)	119 (100%)	107 (100)		
Sex					67 (56.3%)	68 (63.5%)	52 (43.6%)	39 (36.4%)	119 (100%)	107 (100%)				
Educational Qualification			*Below Graduates*		*Graduates*		*Post Graduates*		*Professional Graduates & Vocl. Diploma Holders*		*Total*			
			31 (26.0%)	22 (20.5%)	39 (32.7%)	28 (26.1%)	35 (29.4%)	38 (35.5%)	14 (11.7%)	19 (17.7%)	119 (100%)	107 (100%)		
Occupation	*Students*		*Teacher*		*Professionals*		*Media Personnel*		*Security Personnel*		*General Administrators*		*Educational Administrators*	
	22 (18.4%)	17 (15.8%)	18 (15.1%)	14 (13.0%)	9 (7.5%)	14 (13.0%)	8 (6.7%)	7 (6.5%)	7 (5.8%)	4 (3.7%)	5 (4.2%)	4 (3.7%)	5 (4.%)	5 (4.6)
	Pvt. Sector Employees		*Public Sector Employees*		*Performing Artists*		*Creative Artists*		*NGO Volunteers*		*Others*		*Total*	
	8 (6.7%)	8 (7.4%)	19 (15.9%)	14 (13.0%)	5 (4,2%)	6 (5.6%)	2 (1,2%)	1 (0.9%)	3 (6.5%)	7 (6.7%)	8 (5.6%)	6 (5.6%)	119 (100%)	107 (100%)

Residence	*Urban*		*Semi Urban*		*Rural*		*Total*	
	61 (51.2%)	26 (24.2%)	29 (24.3%)	51 (47.6%)	29 (24.3%)	30 (28.0%)	119 (100%)	107 (100%)
Place of Birth	46 (38.6%)	15 (14.0%)	35 (29.4%)	48 (44.8%)	38 (31.9%)	44 (41.1%)	100%	100%

Income	*Below Rs. 1000*		*Rs. 1001-5000*		*Rs. 5001-10000*		*Rs. 10000 +*		*No Response*		*Total*	
	1 (0.8)	5 (4.6%)	35 (29.4%)	28 (26.1%)	47 (39.4%)	36 (33.6%)	10 (8.4%)	19 (17.7%)	26 (21.8%)	19 (17.7%)	119 (100%)	107 (100%)

Religion	*Hindu*		*Others*		*Total*	
	112 (94.1%)	89 (83.1%)	7 (5.8%)	18 (16.8%)	119 (100%)	107 (100%)

'urban', the periphery of the city which come under the category of 'greater Imphal' may be looked at as 'urban', 'semi-urban' and even in some cases as 'rural'. We have not gone into very strict official classification of these categories and have rather relied on our own common sense perception.

Linguistic Competence – Total and Comparative

By now it has become almost a commonly accepted fact that no community or group is monolingual; hence it is not surprising that literally hundred percent of our respondents are bilingual.

In fact, we took care to select respondents who would know at least English, in addition to their mother tongues. We also wanted to know if the respondents knew and used languages other than their mother tongues and English. Hence in addition to the question on mother tongue, we wanted the respondents to indicate / list the additional languages they knew in order of proficiency in these languages. We have found that all the respondents from Assam have Assamese as their mother tongue and all those from Manipur have Manipuri (Meiteilon) as their

Table 2A: Linguistic Competence (in order of proficiency)

Order of	*Languages*			
proficiency	*English*	*Hindi*	*Bengali*	*Other languages*
1	152 (67.2%)	40 (17.6%)	17 (7.5%)	1 (0.4%)
2.	51 (22.5%)	129 (57.0%)	12 (5.3%)	2 (0.8%)
3.	15 (6.6%)	34 (15.0)	37 (16.3%)	14 (6.1%)
No response	8 (3.5%)	23 (10.1%)	160 (70.7%)	209 (92.4%)
Total	226 (100%)	100%	100%	100%

Table 2B: Linguistic Competence (in order of proticiency)

Order of proficiency	Language							
	English		Hindi		Bengali		Other languages	
	Assam	Manipur	Assam	Manipur	Assam	Manipur	Assam	Manipur
1	70 (58.8%)	82 (76.6%)	29 (24.3%)	11 (10.2%)	17 (14.0%)	0	0	1 (0.9%)
2	31 (26.0)	20 (18.6%)	64 (53.7%)	65 (60.7%)	12 (10.0%)	0	0	2 (1.8%)
3.	11 (9.2%)	4 (3 7%)	13 (10.9)	21 (196%)	31 (260%)	6 (5.6%)	2 (1.7%)	12 (11.1%)
No response	7 (5.8%)	I (0.9%)	13 (19.6%)	10 (26.0%)	59 (5.6%)	101 (1.7)	17 (1.7%)	9:2 (85.9%)
Total	119 (100%)	107 (100%)	100%	100%	100%	100%	100%	100%

mother-tongue. Even though both Assam and Manipur are multilingual states we did not want to complicate our study by taking as respondents people whose mother-tongues were other than Assamese and Manipuri. On the whole Tables 2A and 2B represent the total and comparative figures of individual as well as societal multilingualism. They do not infect represent a complete picture of multilingualism of either Assam or Manipur since we have taken only one language community in each state.

Looking at Table 2A, it can be clearly surmised that English is at the top both in terms of absolute numbers as well as the level of proficiency, as an additional language. Out of the total of 226, 152 (67.2%) respondents have listed English as their first additional language and first in the order of proficiency, another 51(22.5%) have indicated English as the 2nd in order and 15(6.6%) have listed it as the 3rd in terms of proficiency. Quite unexpectedly, 8 (3.5%) of the respondents have not listed English as an additional language. We may mention here that these 8 respondents did not have the required proficiency in English to fill-out the questionnaires; what we had to do was to translate the questionnaire item-wise into the mother-tongue of the respondents and fill out the questionnaire by translating the respondents' responses into English by ourselves. Quite amazingly, some other respondents too could not comprehend the meaning of the terms such as 'spouse', 'colonial-legacy' etc. This may be interpreted as a lexical/semantic problem or a problem of lack of acquaintance with the register of questionnaire survey.

In spite of all these hiccups English has clearly emerged as the most important additional language. No doubt, the figures and the responses cannot be taken as reflective of actual proficiency in English, but they certainly reflect the self-confidence or subjective perception of the respondents. It may also be reflective of the identity function of English in these societies, that is the value, prestige and status attached to this language by the respondents.

Hindi emerges as the second additional language quite closely following English, though only 40(17.6%) of the

respondents have put it as the first in order of proficiency. Another 129(57.0%) and 34(15.0%) have put Hindi in the second and third in order of proficiency respectively. Even though we cannot come to any definite conclusion at this stage, we cannot deny the fact that Hindi seems to be emerging as a close competitor to English as a total of 203 respondents have reported same degree of proficiency in Hindi as compared to 218 in English. It is necessary to relate these responses on language proficiency of the responses to questions on language use in relation to domain, topic and role-relationship in order to get a clearer picture of the relative position of Hindi and English.

Bengali emerges as a poor third with 86 respondents reporting some amount of proficiency in it, while another 17 have reported low level of proficiency in languages such as Nepali, Urdu, Japanese, Telegu, Tamil, Burmese etc. (we have categorised all of them as 'Other Languages'. Looking comparatively at the responses from Assam and Manipur in Table 2B, we find a higher reported proficiency in English from the Manipuri-speaking respondents than the Assamese-speaking respondents both in absolute numbers as well as in order of proficiency. While out of 106 (99.05) respondents from Manipur who have reported proficiency in English as an additional language, a surprising 82(76.6%) have put it in the first order followed by 20(8.6%) and 4 (3.7%) in the second and third order respectively. On the other hand out of the total of 112 respondents from Assam 70(58.5%), 31 (26.0%) and 11 (9.2%) have ranked their proficiency in English in the first, second and third order of proficiency respectively.

With regard to proficiency in Hindi the responses from Assam and Manipur are more or less comparable even though 29(24.3%) respondents from Assam have put Hindi in the first order of proficiency as compared to 11 (10.2%) from Manipur. Further, while Bengali is clearly a third additional language in Assam for socio-historical reasons described in Chapter – 3, there is no clear cut third additional language in the case of Manipur.

Summarising the reported linguistic competence in additional

languages, English is clearly at the top followed by Hindi and Bengali in Assam, and Hindi and 'Other Languages' in Manipur. However as we have already pointed out, these figures simply represent self-reported proficiency which need not correspond to the actual linguistic competence of the respondents. Moreover this kind of a de-contextualised quantification of multilingual competence is of doubtful analytical value unless they are co-related and cross-checked with various socio-linguistic variables.

Medium of Self-education – Total & Comparative

Table 3A represents the information given by the respondents with regard to the medium of instruction at different levels (school, college and university) for their own education. In general, we find that, a vast majority, that is more than 70% of the respondents, began their schooling in their respective mother-tongues, but as they moved up the educational ladder English dramatically takes over the role of the mother-tongues. While 160 (70.7%) had their schooling in the mother-tongue another 44 (14.4%) have reported English medium schooling. It is interesting to note that 19(8.4%) respondents reported a mixed code (mother-tongue and English) and another 3 (1.3%) reported Hindi and English to be the medium of instruction in their school. From our participatory observation, we can definitely assert that these mix-code are used in English medium schools rather than in the mother-tongue medium schools. It may be noted that most of the teachers in English medium schools, whether they are missionary, private or government, do not have the adequate competence to carry out their work exclusively in English for classroom instructions and management and for glossing difficult vocabulary items. They constantly switch over to the mother-tongue of the learner. As a matter of fact, the use of the learner's mother-tongue / the local vernacular reached such a high missionary school in Manipur that the school authorities had to strictly officially prohibit the use of the mother-tongue within the school premises.

Table 3A
Medium of Self-Education (Total)

Languages	*Levels*		
	School	*College*	*University*
Mother-tongue	160 (70.7%)	11 (4.8%)	7 (3.0%)
English	44 (19.4%)	147 (65.0%)	92 (40.7%)
Mother-tongue and English	19 (8.4%)	39 (17.2%)	3 (1.3%)
English and Hindi	3 (1.0%)	0	0
Total	226(100%)	100%	100%

Table 3B
Medium of Self-Education (Comparative)

Languages	*Levels*					
	School		*College*		*University*	
	Assam	*Manipur*	*Assam*	*Manipur*	*Assam*	*Manipur*
Mother-tongue	107 (89.9%)	53 (49.5%)	11 (9.2%)	0	7 (5.8%)	0
Engish	10 (8.4%)	34 (31.7%)	62 (52.1%)	85 (79.4%)	44 (36.9%)	48 (44.8%)
Mother-tongue and English	1 (0.8)	18 (16.85)	29 (24.3%)	10 (9.3%)	2 (1.6%)	1 (0.9%)
English and Hindi	1 (0.8%)	2 (1.8%)	0	0	0	0
No response	0	0	17 (14.2%)	12 (11.2%)	66 (55.4%)	58 (54.2%)
Total	119 (100%)	107 (100%)	100%	100%	100%	100%

With regard to collegiate education 147 (65%) of the respondents reported English while 11 (4.8%) 'mother-tongue' and another 39(17.2%) reported a mixed code of mother tongue and English. It is clear that mother-tongue and English codes–switching has been a common practice in college education not only in North-East but throughout India, specifically in non-urban, non-elite colleges.

It is a bit surprising that 11 (4.8%) respondents have reported mother-tongue to be the medium of college education. Similarly, while 99(40.7%) of the respondents reported English, 07(3.0%) and 3 (1.3%) reported mother tongue and English code-switching for university level of education. This clearly is understandable on our part. It is worth pointing out that, in popular perception in North-east, only those who go for post-graduate studies in the university campuses can and do claim to have university education.

From Table 3B we can make some interesting observations by comparing the figures from Assam with Manipur. In Assam, school education can be seen as the exclusive monopoly of MT medium but in Manipur it is shared in different degree by MT (59.5%), English (31.77%) and MT and English code switching (16.7%). At the college level 11(9.2%) from Assam have reported MT as the medium of education as contrasted with none in Manipur, even though in both the states the official medium of education at the college and university levels is English. Another 7 (5.8%) respondents from Assam reported MT as the medium of instruction at the university level, which we find quite unexplainable. Coming to English, the figures for college and university levels are 62 (52.1%) and 44 (36.9%) for Assam and 85 (79.4%) and 48 (44.8%) for Manipur respectively. Clearly, at higher levels of education, English is the dominant language of education. If the figures appear to be low at these levels it is so because many respondents did not have university education. Another remarkable finding is that as many as 29 (24.3%) respondents from Assam have reported MT and English code-switching in college education. Thus, if English medium higher education is growing from strength to strength in these states,

mother-tongue is encroaching in to what used to be an exclusive domain of English about 2-3 decades ago. Overall, in the education scenario English seems to have a much greater pre-dominance at all levels in Manipur as compared to Assam.

It may be worthwhile to compare the figures for self education with that of the respondents children's education (schooling)

Table 4A: Relative Proficiency in Mother-tongue and English

Skills	*Levels*	*Mother-tongue*	*English*
Listening	Good	221 (97.7%)	141 (62.3)
	Average	5 2.2%)	82 (36.2)
	Poor	0	3 (1.3%)
Speaking	Good	221 (97.7%)	88 (38.9%)
	Average	5 (2.2%)	112 (49.5%)
	Poor	0	26 (11.5%)
Reading	Good	213 (94.2%)	160 (70.7%)
	Average	8 3.5%)	62 (27.4%)
	Poor	5 (2.2%)	4 (1. 7%)
Writing	Good	202 (89.3%)	118 (52.2)
	Average	18 (7.9%)	91 (40.2%)
	Poor	6 (2.6%)	17 (7.5%)
Total		220 (100%)	100%

Table 4B: Relative Proficiency in Mother-tongue and English

Skills	*Levels*	*Mother-tongue*		*English*	
		Assam	*Manipur*	*Assam*	*Manipur*
Listening	Good	117 (98.3%)	104 (97.1%)	69 (57.9%)	72 (67.2%)
	Average	2 (1.6%)	3 (2.8%)	47 (39.4%)	35 (32.7%)
	Poor	0	0	3 (2.5%)	0
Speaking	Good	117 (98.3%)	104 (97.1%)	29 (24.3%)	59 (55.1 %)
	Average	2 (1.6%)	3 (2.8%)	70 (58.8%)	42 (39.2%)
	Poor	0	0	20 (16.8%)	6 (5.6%)
Reading	Good	117 (98.3%)	96 (89.7%)	78 (65.5%)	82 (76.6%)
	Average	2 (1.6%)	6 (5.6%)	38 (31.9%)	24 (22.4%)
	Poor	0	5 4.6%)	3 (2.5%)	1 (0.9%)
Writing	Good	115 (96.6%)	87 (81.3%)	49 (41.1%)	69 (64.4%)
	Average	3 (2.5%)	15 (14.0%)	58 (48.7%)	33 (30.8%)
	Poor	1 (0.8%)	5 (4.6%)	12 (10.0%)	5 (4.6%)
Total		119 (100%)	107 (100%)	100%	100%

which have been presented in Tables 9A and 9B. Such a comparison might hopefully throw some light on inter-generational changes in terms of preference for language in education. There seems

to be a dramatic fall from 160(70.7%) mother-tongue schooling of the respondents to a paltry 25(20.4%) for their children. The figures for English have risen from 44(19.4%) to 82(67.2%) across just one generation. While the figures for a mixed-code switch medium are more or less comparable, the virtually three to four fold increase in English medium schooling is indicative of the future role of English. More on this later when we come to the responses on questions relating to 'medium of children's education'.

Relative Proficiency – Total and Comparative

Table 4A provides the figures on relative proficiency in mother-tongue and English in terms of the four skills of Listening, Speaking, Reading, and Writing (LSRW) on a three-tier scale, i.e. 'good', 'average' and 'poor'. As expected, the reported proficiency levels in all the four skills – Listening-221 (97.7%), 'speaking'-221 (97.7%), 'Reading'-213 (94.2%) and 'Writing'-202 (89.3%) - quite high. The figures for English are certainly lower than those for the mother-tongue, but, yet quite on the upper side as 141 (62.3%) and 82(36.2%) of the respondents have reported 'good' and 'average' in 'Listening' and another 88(38.9%) 112 (49.5%) reported their proficiency in English to be 'good' and 'average' respectively in 'Speaking'. In the productive skills as well 160 (70.7%) and 62(27.4%) have reported their 'Reading' proficiency in English as 'good' and 'average' while another 118 (52.2%) and 91 (40.2%) have repoted that proficiency in 'Writing' to be 'good' and 'average' in English. On the whole, while this reported proficiency, particularly the high figures in English, could not be reliable linguistically, they do seem to reflect the respondents' own perception of their socio-linguistic competence in the language. If we look at the figures in Table 2A on English 152 (67.2%) of the respondents have put it at the first order of proficiency, but if we take the average of all the four skills reported to have 'good' proficiency in English as per Table 4A, the figures stand at 126 (55.7%). This discrepancy, coupled with the unexpectedly high reported proficiency in English, make these figures much less reliable. How far they are indicative of the actual proficiency in terms of communicative needs within specific sociolinguistic settings remains an empirical question.

Table 5A: Use of English at Home

Relation	*Topics*				
	1. Education Official, Collegue, etc.	*2. Social events Festivals, Ceremonies Elections and Problems in locality etc.*	*3. Family matter marriage, quest, savings, food etc.*	*No response*	*Total*
Grand father	3 (1.3%)	1 (0.4%)	1 (0.4)	221 (97.7%)	226 (100%)
Grand mother	0	2 (0.8%)	3 (1.3%)	221 (97.7%)	100%
Father	22 (9.7%)	7 (3.0%)	8 (3.5%)	189 (83.6%)	100%
Mother	3 (1.3%)	2 (08%)	4 (1.7%)	217 (96.0%)	100%
Spouse	33 (14.6%)	17 (7.5%)	21 (9.2%)	155 (68.5%)	100%
Brothers Sisters	48 (21.2%)	28 (123°0)	23 (10.1%)	127 (56.1%)	100% 100%
Children	66 (292%)	27 (I 1.9%)	31 (137%)	102 (45.1%)	100%
Uncle & aunty	21 (9.2%)	13 (5.7%)	11 (48%)	181 (80.0%)	100%
In-laws	21 (92%)	18 (7.9%)	15 (6.6%)	172 (76.1%)	100%
Any other	23 (10.%)	28 (12.3%)	21 (9.2%)	154 (68.1%	100%

Even as we look at the comparative figures between Assam and Manipur, the proficiency levels in all the four skills are quite high, with two important differences. Firstly, in general the proficiency levels in 'listening' and 'reading' are much higher than in 'speaking' and 'writing'; and secondly, in all the four skills Manipur shows comparatively higher proficiency figures

Table 5B: Use of English at Home

Relation	*1. Education, Official, Collegue, etc*		*2.Social Events, Festivals. Ceremonies, Electons and Problems in locally etc.*		*3. Family matters, marriage, savings, food etc.*		*No response*		*Total quest,*	
	Assam	*Manipur*	*Assam*	*Manipur*	*Assam*	*Manipur*	*Assam*	*Manipur*	*Assam*	*Manipur*
Grandfather	0	3 (2.8%)	0	1 (0.9%)	0	1 (0.9%)	119 (100%)	102 (95.3%)	119 (100%)	107 (100%)
Grandmother	0	0	0	2 (1.8%)	2 (1.6%)	1 (0.9%)	117 (97.1%)	104 (97.1%)	100%	100%
Father	6 (5.0%)	16 (14.9%)	1 (0.8%)	6 (5.6%)	1 (0.8%)	7 (6.5%)	111 (93.2%)	78 (72.8%)	100%	100%
Mother	0	3 (2.8%)	0	2 (1.8%)	1 (0.8%)	3 (2.8%)	118 (99.1%)	99 (92.5%)	100%	100%
Spouse	11 (9.2%)	21 (19.6%)	7 (5.8%)	10 (9.3%)	8 (6.7%)	13 (12.1%)	93 (78.1%)	63 (58,8%)	100%	100%
Brother /Sisters	15 (12.6%)	33 (30.8%)	9 (7.5%)	19 (17.7%)	6 (5.0%)	17 (15.8%)	89 (74.7%)	38 (35.5%)	100%	100%
Children	25 (21.0%)	41 (38.3%)	8 (6.6%)	19 (17.7%)	11 (9.2%)	20 (18.6%)	75 (63.2%)	27 (25.2%)	100%	100%
Uncle & Aunty	7 (8.8%)	14 (13.0%)	3 (2.5%)	10 (9.3%)	3 (2.5%)	8 (7.4%)	106 (89.0%)	75 (70.0%)	100%	100%
In-Laws	7 (5.8%)	14 (13.0%)	7 (5.8%)	11 (10.2%)	4 (3.3%)	11 (10.2%)	101 (84.8%)	71 (66.3%)	100%	100%
Any other	8 (6.7%)	15 (14.0%)	8 (6.7%)	20 (18.6%)	5 (4.2%)	16 (14.9%)	96 (82.3%)	56 (52.3%)	100%	100%

than Assam. How these proficiency figures are related to actual language use and attitudes towards English need to be seen.

In order to look at how far the education through English medium and the perceived proficiency in English were reflective of the actual use of English, we put different sets of questions asking the respondents to indicate the use of English in the 'home' domain involving four generations of role-relations, the use of different languages with different non-familial role-relations, and the frequency of use of English for large number of purposes. The responses received have been presented in a tabular form in Tables 5A and 5B, 6A and 6B and 7A and 7B.

Use of English: A domain configuration

1. *Use of English at Home*

In Table 5A, we find the figures on the use of English at home with the ego's family members such as grand father, grand/mother, father, mother, spouse, brothers and sisters, children, uncle and aunts-in-laws and others involving three different topics relating to

(1) Education, Officials, Colleagues etc;

(2) Social events, festivals, ceremonies, elections and local problems etc.; and

(3) Family matters, marriages, guests, savings, food etc.

What is most disturbing about this Table is that quite a high percentage of the respondents ranging from 45% - 97% have not given any response at all which we can as a participant observer interpet as no use of English. In other words, in the domain of home, even though English has made some inroads, depending on topics and role-relations, there is no doubt that this exogenous language has very little use in the family. It is only with the younger relatives like 'spouse', 'siblings' and 'children' that there is some reported use of English in the home, that too restricted to topics that are formal and, perhaps, social. Comparatively there is no overall significant difference between Assam and Manipur even though the figures for Manipur are on a higher side. As a native of Manipur, the present researcher

Table 6A: Language Use (Societal Bilingualism)

Relations	*Language*						
	English	*No response*	*Mother tongue*	*No response*	*Any other*	*No response*	*Total*
Senior Officials	156 (69.0%)	70 (30.9%)	144 (63/7%)	82 (36.2%)	39 (17.2%)	187 (82.7%)	226 (100%)
Colleagues	95 (42.0%)	131 (57.9%)	206 (91.1%)	20 (8.8%)	46 (20.3%)	180 (79.6%)	100%
Friends	92 (40.7%)	134 (59.2%)	215 (95.1 %)	11 (4.8%)	67 (29.6%)	159 (70.3%)	100%
Visitors	142 (62.8%)	84 (37.1 %)	179 (79.2%)	47 (20.7%)	97 (42.9%)	129 (57.0%)	100%
Neighbours	19 (8.4%)	207 (91.5%)	120 (97.3%)	6 (2.6%)	29 (12.8%)	197 (87.1%)	100%)
Servants	3 (1.3%)	223 (98.6%)	147 (65.0%)	79 (34.9%)	26 (11.5%)	200 (88.4%)	100%

can confidently propose that these relatively higher figures do not in anyway reflect the actual use; rather they are indicative of the status and prestige of these people accord to English.

Use of English as Social Interlocutors

Taking into account multilingualism in Assam as well as Manipur, and considering the multilingual repertoire of our respondents, we wanted to find out the languages used by our respondents with different interlocutors – senior officials, colleagues, friends, visitors, neighbours and servants etc. These interlocutors constitute a cline ranging from senior, elderly and respectful acquaintances to neighbours and servants in terms of inter-personal relationships because it is these categories of people that the respondents are in regular day-to-day communicative contact. In terms of the responses we have received, we may put 'senior officials' and 'visitors' into one category as '+ honorific' and 'colleagues' and 'friends' as 'intimate' or 'neutral', whereas neighbours and servants can be put into category that is – 'honorific'.

Table 6B:
Language Use (Societal Bilingualism)

Relations	*Languages*											
	No response		*English*		*No response*		*Mother tongue*		*No response*		*Any other*	
	Assam	*Manipur*	*Assam*	*Manipur*	*Assam*	*Manipur*	*Assam*	*Manipur*	*Assam*	*Manipur*	*Assam*	*Manipur*
Senior Officials	70 (60.5%)	84 (78.5%)	47 (394%)	23 (214%)	84 (70.5%)	60 (56.0%)	35 (294%)	47 (43/9%)	21 (17.6%)	18 (16/8%)	98 (82.3%)	89 (83.1%)
Colleagues	36 (30%)	59 (55.1%)	83 (697°0)	48 (44.8%)	114 (957%)	92 (85.9%)	5 (4.2%)	15 (14.0%)	29 (24.3%)	17 (15.8%)	90 75.6%	90 841%)
Friends	30 (252°'0)	54 (504%)	81 (68.0°/0)	52 (49.5%)	115 (96.6%)	100 (93.3%)	4 (3.3%)	7 (6.6%)	43 (36.1%)	24 (224%)	76 (63.8%)	83 (77.5%)
Visitors	70 (588°0)	72 (67.2%)	49 (41.J00)	35 (327%)	101 (84.8%)	78 (728~o)	18 (15.1%)	29 (27.1%)	61 (51.2%)	36 (33.6%)	58 (48.7%)	71 (66.3%)
Neighbours	7 (58°0)	12 (11.2%)	112 (94.1°0)	95 (88.7%)	1\8 (99.1%)	102 (95.3~0)	I (0.8%)	5 (4.6%)	16 (13.4%)	13 (121%)	1\3 (86.5%)	94 (87.8%)
Servants	0	3 (2.8%)	0	104 (971%)	71 (59.6%)	76 (710%)	49 (40.3%)	31 (28.9%)	13 (10.3%)	13 (121%)	106 (89.0%)	94 (87.8%)
Total	119 (100%)	107 (100%)	100°0	100%	100%	100%	100%	100%	100%	100%	100%	100%

In terms of language choice, English emerges almost at par with the mother tongue, which indicates that all these categories of people belong to virtually the same ethnolinguistic community. Significant difference of course can be found in the category 'colleagues' and 'friends' in which case use of mother-tongue 206(91.1%) and 215 (95.1%) is much higher than the use of English which is reported to be 42.0% and 40.7% respectively. The figures of English with regard to neighbours and servants come down drastically and mother tongue takes almost total predominance because for belongingness to the same ethnolinguistic community as well as social network. The figures of the use of mother/tongue with servants (147 (65.0%)) is lower not because of the use of some other language use but because the practice of keeping servants as domestic helps is restricted to elite families only. The most interesting finding seen in Table 6A is in terms of the figures under the category 'any' Other Language' which happens to be almost 80to 90 percent Hindi. Hindi clearly has found a permanent place in the speech repertoire of the communities as well as individuals. The highest figures for Hindi is in relation to the 'visitors' indicates that such visitors do not speak the mother tongue of the respondents nor are they socially fluent in English. Hindi, therefore, is the clear common choice of communication.

Looking at the comparative figures in Table 6B, we again find a higher use of English in Manipur as compared to Assam, even though there is no dramatic change in figures. The significant point about this Table is not so much in terms of English but rather in terms of Hindi. While it was expected that in Manipuri where no mainstream Indian language has had historical dominance, it was natural for Hindi to occupy the additional space of communication in non-English contexts. However, with regard to Assam, given the century old dominance of Bengali language and linguistic affinity between Assamese and Bengali we expected Bengali to emerge as the most preferred additional language of communication with non-English and non-mother tongue interlocutors. Very surprisingly, however Bengali has been reduced to a minimal role and Hindi, though representing quite low figures seems to be entering the Assamese speech

Table 7A: Use of English (Frequency and Purposes)

Purposes	*Frequency*				
	Regularly	*Sometimes*	*Never*	*No Response*	*Total*
Occupation	83 (36.7%)	123 (54.4%)	9 (3.9%)	11 (4.8%)	226 (100%)
Education	119 (52.6%)	95 (42.0%)	1 (0.4%)	II (4.8%)	100%
Official	131 (57.9%)	83 (36.7%)	8 (3.5%)	4 (17%)	100%
Marketing	8 (3.5%)	130 (57.5%)	80 (35.3%)	8 (3.5%)	100%
Recreation	8 (3.5%)	113 (50.0%)	95 (420%)	10 (4.4%)	100%
Counting	122 (53.9%)	86 (38.0%)	13 (5.7%)	5 (22%)	100%
Abusing	15 (6.6%)	138 (61.0%)	62 (27.4%)	11 (48%)	100%
Joking	9 (3.9%)	127 (56.1%)	82 (36.2%)	8 (3.5%)	100%
Singing	9 (3.9%)	92 (40.7%)	119 (525%)	6 (2.6%)	100%
Bargaining	6 (2.6%)	90 (39.8%)	121 (53.5%)	9 (3.9%)	100%
Gossiping	6 (2.6%)	105 (46.4%)	103 (455%)	12 (5.3%)	100%
Visiting club	14 (6.1%)	99 (438%)	99 (438%)	14 (6.1%)	100%
Hotels & Restaurant	18 (79%)	167 (738%)	36 (15.9%)	5 (22%)	100%
Social function	12 (53%)	143 (63.2%)	66 (29.2%)	5 (2.2%)	100%
Travelling	40 (17.6%)	161 (71.2%)	22 (9.7%)	3 (1.3%)	100%
Banking	68 (30.0%)	109 (482%)	28 (12.3%)	21 (9.2%)	100%
Praying	11 (4.8%)	43 (19.0%)	146 (64.6%)	26 (11.5%)	100%
Writing letters	71 (31.4%)	103 (455%)	50 (221%)	2 (0.8%)	100%
Personal applications etc Official	190 (84.0%)	27 (11.9%)	6 (2..6%)	3 (1.3%)	100%

community in more pervasive way. Given this understanding, we may expect a greater use of Hindi in both Assam and Manipur in the near future.

Use of English: Frequency and Purposes

Having looked at the respondent's proficiency levels in English and their use of the language with different interlocutors, we shall now look at the relationship between English and field of discourse in Tables 7A and 7B. We listed 17 different 'purposes', ranging from the most intimate and private ones like praying, joking, counting etc. to the formal purposes such as occupation, official, conversation and banking etc., and asked the respondents to indicate whether they used English for these purposes 'regularly', 'sometimes' or 'never'. As we can see in Table 7A, the responses more or less correspond to our expectations, in the sense that for official and institutional purposes as well as for traveling, the use of English is greatly higher than for private, personal and socially informal purposes. However, despite such an apparent mutual reciprocity between the use of English and field of discourse, there are a few strikingly disturbing figures which go beyond our understanding. It is, therefore necessary to examine the responses to each individual category of purposes rather than looking for broad generalizations. Let us take the responses to the first three 'purposes' namely occupation, education and official which broadly come under the formal field of discourse. It is interesting to note that only 83(36.7%), 119 (52.6%) and 131 (57.9%) of the respondents have indicated the use of English for purposes of occupation, education and official matters respectively. Another 123 (54.4%), 95 (42.0%) and 83 (36.7%) respondents have indicated that they used English for these purposes respectively only 'sometimes'. This clearly leads us to an inference that some other language, perhaps the common mother-tongue of the interlocutors is almost equally used alongside English for these purposes. Purposes such as marketing, recreation, bargaining, visiting club, hotels and restaurants, and social function broadly belong to a social field of discourse which is mostly informal and hence the reported regular use of English for these purposes is very marginal and negligible. But it is quite

Table 7B: Use of English (Frequency and Purpose)

Purpose	*Frequency*									
	Regularly		*Sometimes*		*Never*		*No response*		*Total*	
	Assam	*Manipur*	*Assam*	*Manipur*	*Assam*	*Manipur*	*Assam*	*Manipur*	*Assam*	*Manipur*
Occupation	34 (28.5%)	49 (45.7%)	74 (62.1%)	49 (45.7%)	9 (7.5%)	0	2 (1.6%)	9 (8.4%)	119 (100%)	107 (100%)
Education	44 (36.9%)	75 (70.0%)	68 (5.1%)	27 (25.2%)	0	1 (0.9%)	7 (5.8%)	4 (3.7%)	100%	100%
Official	55 (46.2%)	76 (71.0%)	54 (45.2%)	29 (27.1%)	8 (6.7%)	0	2 (1.6%)	2 (1.8%)	100%	100%
Marketing	3 (2.5%)	5 (4.6%)	63 (52.9%)	67 (62.6%)	50 (42.0%)	30 (28.0%)	3 (2.5%)	5 (6.4%)	100%	100%
Recreation	0	8 (7.4%)	57 (47.8%)	56 (52.3%)	59 (49.5%)	36 (33.6%)	3 (2.5%)	7 (16.5%)	100%	100%
Counting	59 (49.5%)	63 (58.8%)	49 (41.1%)	37 (34.5%)	10 (8.4%)	3 (2.8%)	1 (0.8%)	4 (3.7%)	100%	100%
Abusing	4 (3.3%)	11 (10.2%)	80 (67.2%)	58 (54.2%)	32 (26.8%)	30 (28.0%)	3 (2.5%)	8 (7.4%)	100%	100%
Joking	0	9 (8.4%)	62 (52.1%)	65 (60.7%)	55 (46.2%)	27 (25.2%)	2 (1.6%)	6 (5.6%)	100%	100%
Singing	2 (1.6%)	7 (6.5%)	41 (34.4%)	51 (47.6%)	74 (62.1%)	45 (42.0%)	2 (7.6%)	4 (3.7%)	100%	100%

Bargaining	1 (0.8%)	5 (4.6%)	40 (33.6%)	50 (46.7%)	74 (62.1%)	47 (43.0%)	4 (3.3%)	5 (4.6%)	100%	100%
Gossiping	0	6 (5.6%)	56 (47.0%)	49 (45.7%)	60 (50.4%)	43 (40.1%)	1 (2.5%)	9 (8.4%)	100%	100%
Visiting Club	2 (1.6%)	12 (11.2%)	66 (46.2%)	44 (41.1%)	59 (49.5%)	40 (17.1%)	1 (2.5%)	11 (10.2%)	100%	100%
Hotels & Restaurant	3 (2.5%)	15 (14.0%)	94 (78.9%)	73 (68.2%)	21 (17.6%)	15 (14.0%)	1 (0.8%)	4 (3.7%)	100%	100%
Social function	3 (2.5%)	9 (8.4%)	74 (62.1%)	69 (64.4%)	41 (34.4%)	25 (23.3%)	1 (0.8%)	4 (3.7%)	100%	100%
Travelling	5 (4.2%)	35 (32.7%)	96 (80.6%)	65 (60.7%)	16 (13.4%)	6 (5.6%)	2 (1.6%)	1 (0.9%)	100%	100%
Banking	34 (28.5%)	34 (31.7%)	60 (45.7%)	49 (14.2%)	17 (10.2%)	11 (10.2%)	8 (6.7%)	13 (12.1%)	100%	100%
Praying	2 (1.6%)	9 (8.4%)	14 (11.7%)	29 (27.1%)	81 (68.0%)	65 (60.7%)	22 (18.4%)	4 (3.7%)	100%	100%
Personal writing letters, appli-cations etc.	13 (0.9%)	58 (54.2%)	65 (54.6%)	38 (35.5%)	40 (33.6%)	10 (9.3%)	1 (0.8%)	1 (0.8%)	100%	100%
Official writing letters, appli-cations etc.	94 (78.9%)	96 (89.7%)	18 (15.1%)	9 (8.4%)	6 (5.1%)	0	1 (0.8%)	2 (1.8%)	100%	100%

unexplainable that such a high percentage of the respondents have reported the use of English 'sometimes' for these purposes.

As a participant observer, I find it quite mysterious to see that 90(30.9%), 99(43.8%), 167(73.8%), 105 (46.4%), and 43(63.2%) respondents used English reported that they 'sometimes' for purposes such as 'bargaining', 'visiting club', 'hotels and restaurants', 'gossiping' and 'social functions' respectively. We know very clearly that both in Assam as well as in Manipur it is by and large the local vernacular speaking markets that our respondents go for marketing and indulge in bargaining, and in such places there is very little scope for the use of English, except, perhaps for just one or two vocabulary items. Again for 'recreation', 'visiting club', 'hotel and restaurant' etc., it is predominantly the local language or a smattering of Hindi that is the norm and one would find same amount a bit of code-mixing with English. 'Social functions' in these two states, especially in the localities and townships where we conducted our field survey, are mostly vernacular oriented. To find that 143(63.2%) of the respondents have reported the use of English ('sometimes') in the field of social functions is totally unreliable. Even for personal, private, extremely intimate purposes such as 'abusing', 'joking', 'singing', 'gossiping' and 'praying' the reported 'regularly' and 'sometimes' use of English, though actually very low, is again quite unexpected and uninterruptible. The most disturbing response is for the purpose of 'counting' where 122(52.9%), 86(38.8%) have reported the use of English 'regularly' and 'sometimes'.

Looking at Table 7B we find it more intriguing to see that the overall reported use of English for all the purposes is higher in the case of Manipur than that of Assam. Since we find the figures in Table 7A as well as 7B to be unreliable and uninterruptible, we can only suggest that this is an area which requires separate study in its own right. An explanation which we may perhaps hesitantly offer is that, given the increasing market as well as social value of English, there is an artificial tendency to report highly inflated but non-existent use of English.

Going into the written mode we had a question asking our

respondents to indicate whether they use English in writing letters, applications etc. Evidently their use of English in the official field of discourse is much higher than the use of English in the personal fields of discourse. Again the figures for Manipur are comparatively higher than those of Assam. Interestingly out of the total 50(22.1%) who reported that they never used English in writing personal letters, 40(33.6%) are from Assam and 10(9.3%) are from Manipur. The fact that 27(11.9%) have reported that they used English in writing letters and applications etc. is ambiguous in the sense that either they write such letters only 'sometimes' or they used English 'sometimes' and some other language 'sometimes'.

Use of English in Media: Print & Electronic

In the next section, we wanted to know the use of and exposure to English through various media which may be broadly divided in to the 'Print Media' (newspapers, journals and magazines) and the 'electronic media' (radio and Television), We also have included 'films' which is perhaps unique and quite different from the rest of the media in the sense that it is an institution that has great social attraction and influence but which at the same time provides an amount of freedom of choice to the viewers. In fact, only when an individual is highly motivated and is prepared to spend time and money that he/she will go for watching a movie in a theatre or in a cinema hall.

As we can see from Table 8A, 124(54.8%) and 81 (35.8%) of the respondents read newspapers, journals and magazines 'regularly' and 'sometimes' respectively. These figures are not very surprising because English language print media has clearly better coverage and higher reliability than the vernacular language media. It would be naive on our part, however, to arrive at any definite conclusion with regard to English versus local language newspapers, journals etc. since our data is restricted to English only. There is no doubt that during the last couple of decades the vernacular media has gained greatly in terms of local readership because of its very specific local news. Therefore, one would, presume that keen readers would go for English as well as for local language(s) in print media.

Table 8A: Use English in Media

Purpose	*Frequency*				
	Regularly	*Sometimes*	*Never*	*No response*	*Total*
Newspaper, journals, magazines	124 (54.8%)	81 (35.8%)	21 (9.2%)	0 (100%)	226
Radio programmes	35 (15.4%)	116 (51.3%)	72 (31.8%)	3 (1.3%)	100%
TV Programmes	72 (31.8%)	144 (63.7%)	9 (3.9%)	1 (0.4%)	
Films	37 (16.3%)	158 (69.9%)	29 (12.8%)	2 (0.8%)	100%

Radio, that was once the opium of the masses, has been greatly replaced by television. Yet from our figures it seems that television has not been able to completely wipe out radio as 35(15.4%) and 116(51.3%) of the respondents reported listening to radio 'regularly' and 'sometimes'. Coming to the most powerful media of to-day (i.e. television), we find that 72 (31.8%) and 144 (63.7%) of the respondents have reported watching television 'regularly' and 'sometimes'.

What is a bit intriguing in these figures is our understanding that the state controlled television as well as the cable television network are more known for propagating Hindi and other dominant language programmes which are mostly film-based and populist. So, this high reporting of watching English language television programmes may be restricted to very limited viewing of news and some other programmes of special interest. Unless we compare these figures with the corresponding figures for Hindi and local language programmes for television, it will be difficult to conclude anything. The same perhaps holds true for films as well since figures for viewing English movies in theatres is not necessarily exclusive of Hindi and local language films.

As with other questions relating to the use of English, here in the case of use and exposure through the print and electronic media as well as watching films etc., the figures for Manipur,

Table 8B

Use English in Media

Purpose	*Frequency*									
	Regularly		*Sometimes*		*Never*		*No response*		*Total*	
	Assam	*Manipur*	*Assam*	*Manipur*	*Assam*	*Manipur*	*Assam*	*Manipur*	*Assam*	*Manipur*
Newspaper, Journals, magazines	55 (46.2%)	69 (64.4%)	51 (42.8%)	30 (28.0%)	13 (10.9%)	8 (7.4%)	0	0	119 (100%)	107 (100%)
Radio programmes	9 (7.5%)	26 (24.2%)	60 (504%)	56 (52.3%)	48 (40.3%)	24 (22.4%)	2 (1.6%)	1 (0.9%)	100%	100%
TV programmes	30 (25.2)	42 (39.2%)	83 (69.7%)	61 (57.0%)	6 (5.0%)	3 (2.8%)	0	1 (0.9%)	100%	100%
Films	7 (5.8%)	30 (28.0%)	87 (73.1%)	71 (66.3%)	24 (20.1%)	5 (4.6%)	1 (.9%)	1 (.9%)	100%	100%

Table 9A: Medium of Children's Education

Medium	*Yes*	*No Response*	*Total*
Mother-tongue	25 (20.4%)	97 (79.5%)	122 (100%)
English	82 (67.2%)	40 (32.7%)	100%
Mother-Tongue & English	12 (9.8%)	110 (90.1 %)	100%
English & Hindi	3 (2.4%)	119 (97.5%)	100%

Table 9B: Medium of Children's Education

Medium	*Yes*		*No Response*		*Total*	
	Assam	*Manipur*	*Assam*	*Manipur*	*Assam*	*Manipur*
Mother-tongue	19 (34.5%)	6 (8.9%)	36 (65.4%)	61 (91.3%)	55 (100%)	67 (100%)
English	31 (56.3%)	51 (76.1%)	24 (43.6%)	16 (23.8%)	100%	100%
Mother-tongue & English	5 (9.0%)	7 (10.4%)	50 (90.9)	50 (89.5%)	100%	100%
English & Hindi	0 (4.4%)	3 (100%)	55 (95.5%)	64	100%	100%

are definitely higher than those for Assam. It is worthwhile to note that in Imphal the capital city of Manipur English films virtually run parallel to Hindi films while in Guwahati or in Assam in general, English movies do not occupy such a strong position. Moreover, due to lack of capital and technological knowhow very few films in Manipur are produced. Thus both the exogenous languages, Hindi and English, have come to monopolise the entertainment space through the electronic media as well as the films to a much greater extent in Manipur than in Assam.

Medium of Children's Education

1. Total & Comparative

We have already passingly commented on the preference for the medium of children's education while discussing about the respondents own education in Table 3A. Now in Table 9A we find that an overwhelmingly 82(67.2%) of the respondents have chosen English medium education for their children as compared to 25(20.4%) for mother tongue medium of education. The comparative figures presented in Table 9B clearly show that there is substantially higher preference for English medium education in Manipur than in Assam. In fact, during the last two to three decades, English medium schools, which were more or less restricted to tribal dominated hills and the urban pockets in Manipur valley, have now mushroomed throughout the state even in very backward and rural areas.

Here, perhaps, we observe a replacive kind of situation in which English medium schools are taking away children from the Manipuri medium schools, Only those who cannot efford the expenses of meeting exorbitant fees and other related expenses for the privately run English medium schools are forced to send their wards to Manipuri medium schools. There is hardly any evidence of even a single parent sending his/her ward for mother-tongue medium education by conscious choice and preference. This is a very alarming situation as it has serious sociolinguistic implications for the future of these societies. It may be noted here that the figures in Tables 9A and 9B represent 122 out of the total 226 respondents who reported to have school going children. It is out of these 122 that we have counted the numbers and percentages for different languages. Lastly, though we do not have figures for different levels of education or even the different levels for schooling, we can overall, observe that there is a dramatic move towards English medium schooling in a temporal context of just one generation. To make further advance in this area, we require a good amount of longitudinal data to grasp the complex pattern of intergenerational changes in the language of schooling.

Table 10A: Reasons for Choosing English Medium School

Reasons	*Yes*	*No*	*No opiniun*	*No response*	*Total*
I want my child to be proficient in English	76 (62.2%)	2 (1.6%)	5 (4.0%)	39 (31.9%)	122 (100%)
for higher education	73 (59.8%)	I (08%)	4 (32%)	44 (36.0%)	100%
for better employment	73 (59.8%)	4 (3.2%)	6 (4.9%)	39 (31.9%)	100%
for social status and prestige	40 (32.7%)	11 (9.0%)	13 (10.6%)	58 (47.5%)	100%
for business and economic activity	43 (352%)	12 (9.8%)	15 (12.2%)	52 (42.6%)	100%

Reason for Choice of Medium

In the questionnaire we had a question asking the respondents, who had sent their children to English medium schools to specify the reasons for doing so. We could not have asked the similar question for the respondent's self education since in traditional societies like Assam and Manipur, almost all decisions regarding schooling of young children are taken unilaterally by the parents. However, this question indirectly probes into the issue of whether the respondents examined consequences of sending their words to school with different mediums of instruction or did they simply went by the prevalent trends. It is clear that more than 40 percent of the respondents who have either expressed no opinion or have not given any response have not thought about the issue seriously and have simply sent their children to English medium schools, perhaps in an ideologically neutral way or by following the dominant trend. It is thus not very surprising to see in Table 10A that 76(62.2%), 73(59.8%) and 73(59.8%) of the respondents have chosen English medium schooling for reason like 'for proficiency in English', 'for higher education' and 'for better employment' respectively. These three reasons are directly related to one

Table 10B: Reasons for Chooing English Medium School

Reasons	Yes		No		No opinion		No response		Total	
	Assam	*Manipur*	*Assam*	*Manipur*	*Assam*	*Manipur*	*Assam*	*Manipur*	*Assam*	*Manipur*
to be proficient In English	25 (45.4%)	5 1 (76.1%)	0	(2.9%)	1 (1.8%)	4 (15.9%)	29 (52.7%)	10 (14.9%)	55 (100%)	67 (100%)
for higher education	38 (690%)	35 (52.2%)	0	1 (1.4%)	0	4 (5.9%)	17 (30.9%)	27 (40.2%)	100%	100%
for better employmcnt	28 (50.9%)	45 (67.1%)	1 (1.8%)	3 (5.4%)	1 (1.8%)	5 (7.4%)	25 (45.4%)	14 (20.8)%	100%	100%
for social status and prestige	15 (27.2%)	25 (37.3%)	3 (5.4%)	8 (11.9%)	3 (5.4%)	10 (14.9%1	34 (61.8%)	24 (35.8%)	100%	100%
for business & economic activity	15 (27.2%)	28 (41.7%)	4 (7.2%)	8 (11.9%)	2 (3.6%)	13 (19.4%	34 (61.8%)	18 (26.8%)	100%	100%

another for it is clear that in the present context a reasonable proficiency in English can only guarantee a better higher education which in turn is a gatepass to better employment. Considering the recent developments of market economy and globalization in India, English has come to play a great role in business and economic activity, replacing the traditional vernacular based trade and commence. Thus when 43 (35.2%) of the respondents report the reason for English medium schooling to be 'for business and economic activity', it sounds quite normal and expected. We are sure that the figures for this particular reason in more modern mainstream urban centres would be much higher. Lastly, whether consciously or unconsciously, it is accepted fact most educated people belonging to a modern society do send their children to English schools for the social status and prestige it commands. Yet, only 40 (32.7%) of our respondents have supported this reason, while 11 (9.0%) have completely denied it. This is probably reflective of a paradoxical situation when parents privately know or are aware of the socioeconomic power of English but are not willing to acknowledge it publicly (cf. Nadkarni 1989 and Aggarwal 1991). The most important thing to be noted here, that all the five reasons included in this question are overlapping to a great extent in the sense that they compliment rather than exclude each other.

In Table 10B, we observe that the figures for 'no opinion' for respondents belonging to Manipur is higher than that of Assam, while the figures for 'no response' for Assam are higher than those of Manipur. In Manipur, there seems to be a perceived direct link between proficiency in English and better employment without any great emphasis on higher education since 51(76.1%) and 45(67.1%) of the respondents have reported the reasons to be 'proficiency in English' and 'better employment' respectively, while a relatively small number, that is 35(52.2%), have specified the reason to be higher education'. In Assam the emphasis seems to be more on higher education since 38(69.0%) have indicated this reason compared to 25(45.4%) and 28(50.9%) of the respondents who have reported 'proficiency in English' and 'better employment' respectively. The picture is further complicated by the fact that 25(36.3%) and 28(41.7%) of the respondents from Manipur have

reported social status and 'prestige' and 'business and economic activity' respectively to be the reasons for preferring English medium schooling as compare to 15(27.2%) respondents in Assam in both the cases. While there is certainly greater public awareness about the socioeconomic power of English in Manipur, one of the reasons for the high figures in this state could be the sudden boost to international trade in the Indo-Burma border town of Moreh which has brought large numbers of people belonging to different sociolinguistic backgrounds together.

Subjective Perception

Utility and Purposes: Total and Comparative

The penultimate question concerns the subjective perceptions of the respondents with regard to the usefulness, relevance or importance of English language for various purposes and spheres of activity. We need not analyze very deeply to see that the usefulness of English is clearly perceived to very high for utilitarian purposes such as 'education', 'science and technology', 'official work', 'trade and commerce' and 'industry'. Next in the hierarchy came spheres like 'national and social mobility' and the lowest figures emerge for socio-cultural activities such as 'literature', 'cultural' 'development' and 'recreation'. A staggering 222(98.2%) and 214(94.6%) of our subjects have reported the great usefulness of English for education, science and technology. Obviously the perception here is in terms of the inherited colonial pattern of education which has virtually totally replaced the indigenous modes of education. 'Science and technology' today seems to refers to only western technology which is on its way to replace indigenous technology, that has had been much better preserved in North Eastern societies than the rest of India. If the figures for 'industry' is low, it is not because some other language is more useful than English but due to the fact that there is very little industrial development and industrial activity in these states. The figures for 'official work' standing at 96.0 percent to presenting 217 respondents are not at all surprising. Even though in reality the mother tongue is used at lower levels of Government offices, successfully achieving one's goal in government agencies, be it a police station, a revenue office, a civic body or the

secretariat of the state, the use of English certainly outweighs the mother-tongue. Next, though the two terms 'social mobility' and 'national mobility' are too broad, we found that the respondents interpreted them as representing communication within one's own sociolinguistic context and going beyond this sociolinguistic context, mostly outside the state respectively. The respondents who have stressed the usefulness of English for 'national mobility' represent 80.9 percent as compared to 73.0 percent for 'social mobility'. Further analysis provides us more convincing explanation as we interpret both 'social mobility' and 'national mobility' in terms of intercultural communication, one within the state and the other outside the state.

Table 11A: Utility and Purposes: Total and Comparative

Purposes	*Yes*	*No*	*No Opinion*	*No response*	*Total*
Social mobility	165 (73.0%)	24 (10.6%)	37 (16.3%)	0	226 (100%)
National mobility	183 (80.9%)	11 (4.8%)	31 (13.7%)	1 0.4%)	100%
Education	222 (8.2%)	2 (0.8%)	1 (0.4%)	1 (0.4%)	100%
Employment	201 (88.9%)	6 (2.6%)	16 (7.0%)	3 (1.3%)	100%
Trade & commerce	175 (77.4%)	11 (4.8%)	34 (15.0%)	6 (2.6%)	100%
Industry	165 (73.0%)	14 (6.1%)	45 (19.9%)	2 (0.8%)	100%
Literature	154 (68.1%)	18 (7.9%)	50 (22.1%)	4 (1.7%)	100%
Cultural development	108 (47.7%)	48 (21.2%)	67 (29.6%)	3 (1.3%)	100%
Recreation	104 (46.0%)	46 (20.3%)	72 (31.8%)	4 (1.7%)	100%
Official work	217 (96.0%)	1 (0.4%)	7 (3.0%)	1 (0.4%)	100%

Table 11B: Usefulness of English

Purpose	Yes		No		No opinion		No response		Total	
	Assam	Manipur	Assam	Manipur	Assam	Manipur	Assam	Manipur	Assam	Manipur
Social mobility	77 (647%)	88 (82.2%)	17 (14.2%)	7 (6.5%)	25 (21.0%)	12 (11.2%)	0	0	119 (100%)	107 (100%)
National mobility	94 (78.9%)	89 (83.1%)	6 (5.0%)	5 (4.6%)	19 (15.9%)	12 (11.2%)	0	I (0.9%)	100%	100%
Education	117 (98.3%)	105 (98.1%)	1 (0.8%)	1 (0.9%)	I (0.8%)	0	0	1 (0.9%)	100%	100%
Employment	105 (88.2%)	96 (89.7%)	3 (2.5%)	3 (2.8%)	11 (9.2%)	5 (4.6%)	0	3 (2.8%)	100%	100%
Trade &. commerce	92 (77.3⁰0)	83 (77.5%)	7 (5.8%)	4 (3.7%)	20 (16.8%)	14 (13.0%)	0	6 (5.6%)	100%	100%
Industry	87 (73.1%)	78 (72.8%)	8 (67%)	6 (5.6%)	24 (20.1%)	21 (19.6%)	0	2 (1.8%)	100%	100%
Science &. Technology	112 (94.1%)	102 (95.3%)	0	0	7 (58%)	3 (2.8%)	0	2 (1.8%)	100%	100%
Literature	72 (60.5%)	82 (76.6%)	14 (11.7%)	4 (37%)	32 (26.8%)	18 (16.8%)	I (0.8%)	3 (2.8%)	100%	100%
Cultural development	48 (40.3%)	60 (56.0%)	29 (24.3%)	19 (17.7%)	41 (34.4%)	26 (24.2%)	I (0.8%)	2 (1.8%)	100%	100%
Recreation	53 (44.5%)	51 (47.1%)	26 (21.8%)	20 (18.6%)	40 (33.6%)	32 (29.9%)	0	4 (3.7%)	100%	100%
Official work	113 (94.9%)	104	1	0	5 (4.2%)	2 (1.8%	0	I 0.9%	100%	100%

As we come to socio-cultural spheres of activity such as 'literature', 'cultural development' and 'recreation', the figures stand at 154(68.1%), 108 (47.7%) and 104(46.0%) respectively. We can perhaps make a couple of tentative inferences from these figures. First, the high figure of 68 percent for 'literature' is indicative of the fact that, in general, English literature is seen as superior to mother-tongue literature. Secondly, when the figures for 'cultural development' represent 47.7 percent of the total sample, it clearly indicates a tendency to move towards English-oriented, western cultural practices, Even for 'recreation' English is found to be useful by 46.0 percent of the sample while only 20.3 percent have denied the usefulness of English for this purpose. On the whole the notion of domain separation seems to be untenable English not only as a language but also as a cultural symbol and way of life seems to be pervading these societies. To draw an artificial distinction between English as a language of utility representing instrumental function and the mother-tongue as the language of culture and identity seems to be artificial and is not supported by our empirical evidence.

Looking at Table 11B, in terms of subjective perceptions of the usefulness of English in various domains and various spheres of activity the do not seem to be any significant difference between the respondents from Assam and those from Manipur. Of course, the general pattern that has emerged so far in terms of quantitively higher response in favour of English in Manipur as compared to Assam holds true for this question as well. The fact that 11.7 percent of the respondents have denied the importance of English for 'literature' in Assam as compared to 3.7 percent from Manipur is reflective of some kind of a negative self image towards the respective mother-tongues and the corresponding cultures.

The English Problematic: Statement, Attitudes and Subjectivity

The last question in the questionnaire comprises a set of twenty (20) statements asking the respondents to express their agreement, disagreement or no opinion for each of the statements. We have tabulated the responses to this question in Tables 12A

Table 12A: The English Problematic

Statements	*Yes*	*No*	*No Opinion*	*No remarks*	*Total*
1	*2*	*3*	*4*	*5*	*6*
I. I like English	215 (35.1%)	5 (2.2%)	6 (2.6%)	0	226 (100%)
2. English is as useful as Hindi	165 (73.0%)	37 (16.3%)	19 (8.4%)	5 ((2.2%))	100%
3. I encourage my children to learn and use English	217 (96.0%)	2 (0.8%)	4 (1.7%)	3 (1.3%)	100%
4. English language is responsible creating divisions in our family	21 (9.2%)	168 (74.3%)	36 (15.9%)	1 (0.4%)	100%
5. I can express myself best in English	84 (37.1%)	100 (44.2%)	41 (18.1%)	1 (0.4%)	100%
6. English is essential for good administration	142 (62.8%)	37 (163%)	46 (20.3%)	1 (0.4%)	100%
7. English is a mark of colonial legacy	60 (26.5%)	90 (39.8%)	74 (32.7%)	2 (0.8%)	100%
8. English is as important as my mother-tongue	145 (64.1%)	55 (24.3%)	24 (10.6%)	2 (0.8%)	100%
9. We cannot achieve industrial development without English	124 (54.8%)	49 (21.6%)	51 (22.5%)	2 (22.5%)	100%
10. Englishis the main reason for social inequality	39 (12.2%)	132 (58.4%)	55 (24.3%)	0	100%
11. English is essential for national unity and integrity	122 (53.9%)	54 (23.8%)	49 (21.6%)	1 (0.4%)	100%
12. Because of English our children cannot do well in edn.	78 (34.5%)	123 (54.4%)	22 (9.7%)	3 (1.3%)	100%

Statement					
13. English is destroying our society because it promotes western life style	32 (14.1%)	162 (71.6%)	32 (14.1%)	0	100%
14. It is impossible to live without English	34 (15.0%)	167 (73.8%)	25 (11.0%)	0	100%
15. The English educated elite is exploiting the common masses	36 (159%)	141 (62.3%)	49 (29.6%)	0	100%
16 The poorer people cannot develop withotu English	27 (11.9%)	158 (69.9%)	41 (18.1%)	0	100%
17. I am proud of English	111 (49.1%)	61 (26.9%)	52 (230%)	2 (08%)	100%
18. English is the only feasible linked languge in India	94 (41.5%)	99 (43.8%)	31 (I 3.7%)	2 (0.0%)	100%
19. I am most comfortable while communicating in English	113 (50.0%)	81 (35.6%)	27 (11.9%)	5 (2.2%)	100%
20. The powerful position of English is harmful for the development of my mother-tongue	46 (20.3%)	134 (59.2%)	46 (20.3%)	0	100%

and 12B. We have called it the 'English Problematic' because it deals with the various dimensions of English ranging from the individual respondent's personal feelings and attitudes towards English to the larger questions of the socio-political role of English in India. The 20 statements presented deliberately in a random manner may be organised into 5 more or less related groups. Group A contains 'Statements' No. 1 ('I like English'), 5('I can express myself best in English'), 7('English is a mark of colonial legacy'), 17('I am proud of English') and 19('I am most comfortable while communicating in English'). These 'Statements' directly relate to the respondents' personal feelings and attitudes towards English both as an institution and a communicative tool. At the deeper level, Statements 1 and 17 are relative and

Table 12B:The English Problematic

Statements	Yes Assam	Yes Manipu	No Assam	No Manipur	No opinion Assam	No opinion Manipur	No remarks Assam	No remarks Manipur	Total Assam	Total Manipur\
1	2	3	4	5	6	7	8	9	10	11
1. I Like English	114 (95.70/.)	101 (943%)	I (0.8%)	4 (3.7%)	4 (33%)	2 (1.8%)	0	0	119 (100%)	101 (100%)
2. English is as useful as Hindi	89 (74.7%)	76 (710%)	21 (11.6%)	16 (14.9%)	8 (6.7%)	11 (10.2%)	I (0.8%)	4 (3.1%)	100%	1000%
3. I encourage my children to learn and use English	114 (95.7%)	103 (96.2%)	2 (1.6%)	0	2 (1.6%)	2 (18%)	1 (0.8)	2 (18%)	100%	100%
4. English language is responsible for creating divisions in our family	11 (9.2%)	10 (9.3%)	94 (18.9%)	74 (69.1%)	14 (117%)	22 (205%)	0	I	100"1. (09%)	100%
5. I can express myself best in English	34 (285%)	50 (467%)	60 (50.4%)	40 (373%)	25 (21.0%)	16 (149%)	0	I (09%)	100%	100%
6. English is essential for good administration	74 (62.1%)	68 (63.5%)	21 (17.6%)	16 (143%)	24 (201%)	22 (20.5%)	0	I	100% (09%)	100%

(contd...)

1	2	3	4	5	6	7	8	9	10	11
7. English is a mark or colonial legacy	35 (29.4%)	25 (23.3%)	41 (34.4%)	49 (45.7%)	43 (36.1%)	31 (289%)	0	2 (18%)	100%	100%
8. English is as important as my mother-tongue	68 (51.1%)	17 (71.9%)	37 (310%)	18 (16.8%)	13 (10.9%)	11 (10.2%)	1 (0.8%)	1 (0.9%)	100%	100%.
9. We cannot achieve industrial development without English	64 (53.7%)	60 (56.0%)	28 (235%)	21 (196%)	27 (226%)	24 (224%)	0	2 (1.8%)	100%	100%
10. English is the main reason for social in-equality	20 (16.8%)	19 (177%)	61 (563%)	65 (60.7%)	32 (268%)	23 (21 4°/.)	0	0	100%	100%
II. English is Essential for national unity and integrity	60 (50.4%)	62 (57.9%)	35 (25.4%)	19 (17.7%)	24 (20.1%)	25 (23.3%)	0	I (0.9%)	100%	100'
12. Because of English our children cannot do well in edn.	45 (37.8%)	33 (30.8%)	58 (48.7)	65 (60.4%)	15 (12.6%)	7 (6.5%	1 (0.8%)	2 (1.8%)	100%	100%
13. English is destroying our society	15 (12.6%)	17 (158%)	91 (76.4%)	71 (663%)	13 (109%)	19 (111%)	0	0	100%	100%

14.	It is Impossible to live without English	15 (12.6%)	19 (17.7%)	88 (73.9%)	79 (73.8%)	16 (13.4%)	9 (8.4%)	0	0	100%	100%
15.	The English educated elite is exploiting the common masses	20 (16.8%)	16 (14.9%)	75 (630%)	66 (61.6%)	24 (2.1%)	25 (23.3%)	0	0	100%	100%
16.	The poorer people cannot develop without English	9 (75%)	18 (168%)	87 (731%)	71 (663%)	23 (19.3%)	18 (16 8%)	0	0	100%	100%
17.	I am proud of English	58 (48.7%)	53 (49.5%)	33 (277%)	28 (261%)	28 (23.5%)	24 (224%)	0	2 (1.8%)	100%	100%
18	English is the only feasible linked language in India	37 (31.0%)	57 (532%)	64 (537%)	35 (327%)	18 (151%)	13 (121%)	0	2 (1.8%)	100%	100%
19	I am most comfortable while communication in English	48 (40. 3%)	65 (60.7%)	53 (44.5%)	28 (261%)	18 (15.1%)	9 (8.4%)	0	5 (4.6%)	100%	100%
20	The powerful position of English is harmful for the development of my mother-tongue.	23 (193%)	23 (214%)	72 (605%)	62 (579%)	24 (20.1%)	22 (20.5%)	0	0	100%	100%

Statements 5 and 19 are related as versions of same notion, while 7 stands as a criss-cross test against these two sub-groups.

It is interesting to note that while 215 (95.1%) said that 'Yes' to "I like English' only 111 (49.1%) yes to' I am proud of English'. As we go to the Statement 'English is a mark of colonial legacy' only 60(26.5%) respondents agreed with it, but 90(39.8%) of them did not think that English was a mark of colonial legacy and 74(32.7%) had no opinion on this statement. Statements No. 5 ('I can express myself best in English') and 19 ('I am most comfortable while communicating in English') are different versions of the same question asking the respondents about how they felt in using English for communicative purposes. Only 94 (37.1%) agreed with the Statement 5 while 113 (50.0%) agreed that they were most comfortable while using English in communication. This reflects a kind of paradox that exists in the minds of the respondents and such paradoxes inconsistencies and internal contradiction will be observed as we look at the responses to other groups of statements.

Statements 2 ('English is as useful as Hindi'), 8 ('English is as important as my mother-tongue') and 20 ('The powerful position of English is harmful for the development of my mother-tongue') were meant to make the respondents think about English in relation to their mother-tongue and Hindi. Quite contrary to the notion that like many parts of South India in North Eastern India there is a kind of strong anti-Hindi feeling. We find that as many as 165 (73.0%) of the subject thought that Hindi was as useful as English. Further, 145 (64.1%) respondents thought that English was as important as their mother tongue and only 46(20.3%) thought that the powerful position of English is harmful for the development of their mother-tongue as against 134 (59.2%) who did not think that English was detrimental to mother-tongue development. The overall picture that emerges is that a vast majority of our respondents seem to be positively accepting a multilingual situation in which there is no conflict between English versus the mother-tongue or English versus Hindi. If we go by the responses than Verma's (notion) of complementarity of language spoken in India is a network of networks... is quite valid and relevant.

Group C includes two simple Statements- No.3 ('I encourage my children to learn and use English') and No. 12 ('Because of English our children can not do well in education') relate to the pedagogic aspect of English. The contradiction in the respondents' desire in terms of their children's proficiency in English and the meeting of these expectations by the educational institutions is evident in the responses in these two questions. While as high as 217(96.0%) encouraged their children to learn and use English or be more proficient in English. 78 (34.5%) thought that the educational performance of their children suffered because of lack of adequate proficiency in English. Even though we have not probed this aspect in greater detail, it is quite clear that our educational institutions have failed somehow to meet the English language needs and expectations of these parents. It will be worthwhile to explore this gap further in order to understand the English problematic better from the pedagogic point of view.

Statements No.4 ('English language is responsible for creating divisions in our family') and No.13 ('English is destroying our society because it promotes western lifestyle') are related to the cultural implications of English. It is interesting to note that only 21(9.2%) respondents thought that English language created disharmony in the family but as many as 32 (14.1%) thought English language was responsible for promoting western lifestyles. In fact in its cultural dimension, English in North East India is remarkably different from that of mainstream India. Here, there is no negative cynical attitude towards the use of English within the family and there is no negative stereotype with regard to western lifestyle. Perhaps this is indicative a more liberal, egalitarian outlook that the people of North-east are famous for.

Another eight statements which, we have broadly put under group E relate to the socio-political and economic role of English. These 8 Statements are as follows: No. 6. ('English is essential for good administration'), No. 9. ('We cannot achieve industrial development without English'), No. 10. ('English is the main reason for social inequality'), No. 11. ('English is essential for national unity and integrity'), No. 12. ('It is impossible to live

without English'), No. 15. ('The English educated elite is exploiting the common masses'), No. 16. ('The poorer people cannot develop without English') and No. 18. ('English is the only feasible link language of India'). With regard to Statement No. 6 which is related to the role of English in public administration, 142 (62.8%) thought that English language was essential for good administration. This is a bit surprising in view of the fact that in terms of the respondents' own proficiency in English and the lack of any proficiency whatsoever in English that the larger masses of people suffer from, it is quite surprising to note that good public administration could be run in this language. A plausible explanation lies in people's perception of feudal administration in the mother-tongue and the more 'democratic' administration in English. Since the present public administrative system came to both Assam and Manipur, as much as to the rest of North East by dismantling the feudal, exploitative, and arbitrary rule of the Kings, English language administration is viewed positively.

In relation to Statement No. 9., 124 (54.8%) thought that industrial development was not possible without English. Almost similar to the question on administration, here also our respondents seemed to link industrial development to western technology and, therefore, to English language.

Statements No. 10 and No. 15 relate to the question of language and socio-economic as well as political dimentions. Almost similar number of respondents, i.e. No. 132 (58.4%) and No.141 (62.3%) did not think that English caused social inequality and that the English educated elite exploited the common masses respectively. Such an intriguing responses to vital questions of social inequality and exploitation can only be explained in terms of Gramscian notion of 'cultural harmony' or Ngungi's concept of colonisation of mind', where the exploited do not think that they have been exploited. Statement No. 16. further reinforces the relevance of the notion of cultural harmony as 158(69.9%) respondents did not think that the cause of poverty of the poorer sections is due, to their lack of proficiency in English. We will examine this aspect in more detail in the next chapter.

Statements No. 11. and No. 18. relate to the role of English as a 'link language' and its implications for national unity and integrity. Though only 94 (41.5%) of the respondents thought English to be the only feasible link language in India, a greater number, that is 122 (53.9%), thought English to be essential for national unity and integrity. It is quite feasible that both English and Hindi are perceived as link languages, though the controversies surrounding both of these languages do seem to have an impact on the responses of our respondents. Lastly Statement No. 14. is a wild sort of vague statements; 'It is impossible to live without English'. We expected all the respondents to say 'no' to the Statement, but 34 (15.0%) have responded as 'yes' while another 25 (11.0) have expressed 'no opinion'. This certainly adds a tragicomic to the English problematic.

Comparatively we do not find any significant difference in responses from Assam and Manipur. The marginal difference are in terms of responses to Statement No. 5. ('I can express myself best in English') and No. 19. ('I am most comfortable while communicating in English') where the respondents from Manipur display greater communicative confidence in English than the respondents from Assam. There is also a significant difference in responses to Statement No. 18. ('English is the only feasible link language in India') in which case 57(53.2%) respondents from Manipur said 'yes' as compared to 37(31.7%) from Assam.

It may be pointed out here that there is a greater possibility of considering both English and Hindi as parallel link languages in Assam whereas in Manipur people in general would not put Hindi at par with English for this role. Further in response to Statement No. 8. ('English is as important as my mother-tongue') 77(71.9%) respondents from Manipur said 'yes' as compared to 68(57.1%) from Assam. While in both the states there does not exist any conflict or competition between the mother-tongues and English, English certainly has a superior social status in Manipur than in Assam. This is born out of the fact that during the two decade long movement for inclusion of Manipuri in the 8th Schedule of the Constitution of India, there was no anti-

English expression at all, even though sporadic expressions against all major Indian languages, particularly Hindi, was observed. Though we need more data and deeper analysis for an adequate understanding of the English problematic, we clearly, did not observe any hypocritical attitude towards English whereby people hated English publicly but loved it privately.

5

FINDINGS AND CONCLUSION

In this Chapter, we would discuss the major 'findings' and 'conclusions' of the whole study. Even though we have used the term 'conclusion', it is necessary to point out that we arrived at more confounding and complex questions rather than any definitive answers. Therefore, our conclusions are not conclusions at all; rather, they are seeds for further meaningful questions which need to be articulated and addressed systematically. The findings of the study have been drawn from the empirical study. However, during our analysis, interpretations and arriving at the findings, we have drawn heavily on the secondary information presented in Chapter 2 and from our own diary notes, intuitive understanding and an insider's observations. In the following section, we shall sum up our findings and then go on to see if it is possible to relate these findings to the theoretical issues presented in Chapter 1.

The first section of the questionnaire contained questions relating to the social, economic and educational background of the respondents. This has helped us in preparing a general profile of the respondents in simple statistical figures. We need to highlight here, however, the fact, firstly, that these figures can not be compared to similar figures drawn from more advanced states in mainstream India, and, secondly, that they are also not strictly comparable to similar figures from within north-east India itself. For example, what is 'urban' and 'middle class' in a state like Maharastra is far different from what is an 'urban, middle class' gentleman in Imphal or Guwahati. Similarly, what constitutes a 'higher income group' in Guwahati is very different from a similar category in Imphal. Keeping these fundamental

differences in mind, let us now look at the profile of our respondents very briefly.

In terms of 'age', a vast majority of our respondents are in the mid- professional age group ranging from 20 to 50 years. While we have taken younger persons studying in schools and colleges, we also have included about 30% of our respondents in the age group of 41 to 45. In terms of 'sex', even though our sample is not representative with reference to Census figures, we do have an appropriate sample comprising about 60% males and 40% females.

In terms of 'education', we have a more spread out sample ranging from school-and college-going children to post-graduates in general education as well as professionals having Bachelor and Masters degrees in Law, Medicine, Engineering and Technology etc. These respondents, again, represents a cross section of occupational groups, ranging from simple secretarial staff to important political, sports, media and other personalities who do influence society in significant ways. Purposely, we included 39(17.2%) school and college level students as well as 32 (14%) teachers at different levels of education.

Interestingly, while most of our respondents were born in rural and semi-urban areas, most of them have migrated to semi-urban and urban pockets. Again, a vast majority of our respondents belong to the high income group within the parameters of the overall north-east scenario. Of course, religion-wise, an overwhelmingly 89% of our respondents are Hindus while the rest of 11% are Buddhists, revivalists of indigenous religions and atheists. We have found it very difficult to arrive at any meaningful differences between the Assamese and Meetei respondents, though, by and large, they represent the same socioeconomic, and educational background. We have presented the comparative figures in Table-IB.

In the following section, we will look at language competence in terms of the self-reported multilingual repertoires of the individuals. We have also tried to see how these repertoires correlate with language use in different domains for different purposes with different interlocutors and in different modes.

Finally, we have looked at the overt and covert motivations for learning and using English, attaching greater importance to their perception of and reactions towards the role of English in different micro domains and their subjective reactions to a variety of 20 different 'Statements' covering a wide range of social, political, scientific, technological, educational, administrative and related spheres of the use of English.

We had chosen respondents whose mother tongues were Assamese and Manipuri (Meeteilon) in Assam and Manipur respectively and who have had some amount of proficiency in and use of English. All our respondents were at least bilinguals (mother tongue and English) though a large number of then can be categorised as multilingual with knowledge and use of two or more languages.

In terms of ranking proficiency in additional languages, English has clearly emerged at the top, followed by Hindi and a number of other languages. Reportedly, Meeteilon-speakers have much greater proficiency in English than the Assamese mother tongue speakers. It is necessary to point out here that these are self-reported proficiencies which did not necessarily reflect actual proficiency in the languages concerned. They do, however, reflect the ideological productions and their ideological identification with English in the 'Outer' and 'Expanding' Circles of English in Assam and Manipur.

The findings on self-education reveal an intriguingly confusing picture on the surface, both in Assam and in Manipur. On deeper probing, it becomes clear that it is the confusing and conflicting state of affairs in education, in terms of 'medium', that has got reflected in the responses of our respondents. Even though there are officially recognised English medium schools and even though the official medium of higher education is exclusively English in Assam as well as in Manipur, the ground reality is strikingly different.

Again, while looking at the relative proficiencies in one's own mother tongue, the entire picture is confounding. Increasingly, these figures convinced us that it requires a great deal of serious investigations to be able to even articulate the English problematic.

Our study has certainly revealed the subjectivity of the respondents, regarding their own perceptions of the 'range' and 'depth' of English as well as their conscious or subconscious intuitions about the parameters of the 'power' of English.

Use of language in different fields, tenor and modes of discourse can and does reflect a relatively more realistic picture of both competence as well as actual use. The same purpose can be served by working out a domain configuration, with actual recordings of linguistic data and observations. Since analysis of actual linguistic data of language use was not the focus of the present study, we have not collected or analysed any such data. As in the case of language proficiency, in terms of language use also we have looked at the respondents' subjective reporting. We have examined the use of English in different domains such as the home, printed and electronic media as well as official spheres; use of English for different purposes from the strictly personal to socio-cultural and official ones, involving a variety of interlocutors ranging from blood relations to entirely unknown impersonal communicators. The overall picture that has emerged is a greater tendency towards the use of English particularly with younger generations and in the written mode. Hindi certainly has encroached into a number of domains that were earlier meant for mother tongue and English. But, this in no way, affected the amazingly great use of English irrespective of the field, tenor or mode of discourse. Such a tendency is more visible in Manipur as compared to Assam.

We wanted to know the respondents' preferred medium of education for their children. This was done in order to see whether there was any decipherable trend towards a shift from mother tongue to English or vice versa. The findings show the overwhelming preference for English medium education in both the states. Again, the balance has tilted in Manipur towards a greater preference for English, irrespective of the fact that the status of Meeteilon got great boost in the last decade by its inclusion in the Eight Schedule of the Constitution of India. Paradoxically, only some of the Assamese-speaking respondents' reflected preference for mother tongue speaking medium.

Lastly, we have looked at the respondents' subjective attitudes

towards, subjective perceptions and understanding of the role, position, usefulness, power and politics of English in their respective societies as can be seen from the detailed figures presented in Chapter 4 (Tables 11 and 12). The psychological grip of English is more than evident. Virtually, for all purposes, including literary, cultural and recreationary domains, there is a strikingly, or perhaps disturbingly, great preference for English. The last question that contained 20 Statements dealing with various dimensions of English ranging from the individual respondent's likes and dislikes, the role of English in India and the exploitative power or otherwise of the continuance of English in India, has evoked responses that further strengthen the perceived virtually monopolistic dominance of English. Though there are differences in Assam and Manipur, the overall picture that has emerged is a strongly positive role of English without any conflictual positions in terms of English and mother tongue.

The foregoing discussion, including the secondary material presented in Chapter 2 and the findings of the Field Survey in Chapter 4 have important pedagogical implications in terms of English Language Teaching (ELT) in the north-east. One of the crucial observations that can be made here is that no anti-English feeling whatsoever exists in this region of the country. The reason of it is quite clear – North-East India did not experience the kind of British colonial oppression and exploitation which people in most parts of mainstream India had to go through. The arrival of the British rulers in Assam as well as in Manipur was much later than the other parts. Apart from economic interests in the tea gardens of Assam and the forest and the natural sources in Assam and Manipur, there was hardly anything of great significance for the colonial rulers. Additionally, the rulers had learnt not to interfere in any big way in the socioreligious and cultural life of the colonised people. Therefore, there was very little missionary work carried on in the Brahmaputra and Manipur valleys. No doubt, the story of the tribal-inhabited areas in both the state is quite different and is beyond the scope of the present study.

What is of utmost interest pedagogically is the fact that, in both Assam and Manipur, there is a very strong favourable

attitude towards English. The hang-over of colonial rule, found mainly in the Hindi heartland of India, is totally absent in this region. In fact, because of the role played by the Hindi-speaking security forces, there exists very strong anti-Hindi feelings in the region. And, this is more true in the case of Manipur.

The English educated elite in the region appears to be clear about their relationship to English as a language. There is no ambivalance here. They have learnt, use, want to learn and want to use English for very clear instrumental purposes, which include regional and national mobility, pursuit of higher education, better employment opportunities, access to modern knowledge including science and technology and a host of other purposes. There is no observable conflict between one's emotional and symbolic attachment to the mother-tongue and a great attraction for English, the language of success in the global market.

Such an encouraging socio-linguistic setting could have been appropriately exploited by ELT specialists to advance and strengthen the teaching and learning the language both qualitatively as well as quantitatively. Clearly, there has been tremendous quantitative development of English-medium education in the area. That English medium schools have literally mushroomed in the north-east has by now become *cliche*. But, qualitatively, there has been great dilution. Most of the reforms in syllabus design, teacher training programmes and methodological experimentations, recommended by the local as well as national academic bodies have virtually no impact on the traditional grammar-translation method being practiced unceasingly. There has been a shift to 'communicative' and 'interactional' approaches. Unfortunately, all these have remained on paper and as precepts, but hardly reflected in or translated to practice.

English appears to fulfill not only the instrumental function, it as has come to fulfill the communicative and identical functions, as reflected in the subjective perceptions of the people. We have not been able to examine this aspect in any detail. It remains a question unanswered and a question that could be probed into in future research. We, however, do understand that Assam

and Manipur have become integral parts of the 'Outer Circle' of English. The power of English in terms of its grip on the minds of the people is clearly reflected. But the question of the politics of English remains unravelled because it, perhaps, is a question that can be properly looked into in terms of a global context.

As we have pointed out again and again, we have more questions than answers. We hope, we have been able to articulate, with some degree of success, the basic questions relating to the power and politics of English in Assam and Manipur from a socio-pedagogic perspective. These questions may form the basis for further research into the English problematic. If our empirical evidence can help future researchers to problematize specific areas of research, we shall feel amply rewarded. Last but not the least, we need to work out the different ruminations of an interface between theoretical propositions and empirical data. This singularly constitutes the most important area of research for us as well as other researchers in future.

BIBLIOGRAPHY

Achebe,C. 1976. *Morning Yet to Creation Day*. Garden City: Doubleday.

Adorno, T.W., Else, F.B. Levinson, D.J. and Sanford, R.N. 1950. *The Authoritian Personality*. New York: Harper.

Aggarwal, K.S. 1984. *Language Planning: Socio-Economic Factor and Attitudes to English*. M.Litt. Dissertation. Hyderabad: Central Institute of English and Foreign Languages.

Aggarwal, K.S. 1988. English and India's, Three Language Formula: An Empirical Perspective. *World Englishes*, Vol-7, No.3, 288-99

Aggarwal, K.S. 1992. To Include or not to include: An attempt to study the language conflict in Manipur. *Language Problems and Language Planning*. Vol.16, No.1 21-27.

Aggarwal, K.S. 1993. Crisis of Identity: The Linguistic quagmire. *Independent*, 23rd April 1993.

Aggarwal, K.S. 1994. *Language in the Plural context of Imphal: A Multidimensional and Empirical Perspective* Ph.D. Dissertation. New Delhi: Jawaharlal Nehru University.

Aggarwal, K.S. (ed.). 1999. *Dynamics of Identity and Intergroup Relations in North East India*. Shimla: Indian Institute of Advanced Study.

Agnihotri, R. K. Khanna, A.L. and Mukherjee, A. 1983. *Variations in the Use of Tenses in English: A Sociolinguistic Perspective.* (A Report of ICSSR Project) New Delhi: ICSSR.

Agnihotri, R.K. and Khanna, A.L. (ed.). 1994. *Second Language Acquisition: Socio-Cultural and Linguistics Aspects of English in India*. New Delhi: Sage.

Agnihotri, R.K. and Khanna, A.L. (eds.). 1995. *English Language Teaching in India: Issues and Innovations*. New Delhi: Sage.

Agnihotri, R.K. et al (eds.). 1997. *Problematizing English in India*. New Delhi: Sage

Akmajian, A. et al 1995. *Linguistics: An Introduction to Language and Communication*. Cambridge: MIT Press.

Allen, B.C. 1906 *Assam District Gazetteers*. Vol.7, Sibsagar. Allahabad: Pioneer Press

Allen, J. P. B. and Corder, S.P. (eds.). 1973. *Readings for Applied Linguistics: The Edinburgh Course in Applied Linguistics*. Vols. 1-4. London: Oxfords University Press.

Allwood, J. 1976. *Linguistic Communication in Action and Cooperation: A study in pragmatics*. University of Gathernberg.

Andersen, R. (ed.). 1983. *Pidginization and Creolization as Language Acquisition*. Rowely, MA: Newbury House.

Annamalai, E. (ed.). 1979. *Language Movements in India*. Mysore: CIIL

Annamalai, E. 1991. 'Satan and Saraswati: the double face of English in India. *South Asian Language Review*, 1:1. pp. 3343.

Ansari, S.A. 1976. *Economic Geography of Manipur*. Imphal: Trio Book Store.

Appel, R. and Muyksen, B. 1987. *Language Contact and Bilingualism*. London: Edward Arnold.

Apte, M. 1980. *Acquisition of English Syntax by Marathi Learners: An Investigation*. M.Litt Dissertation. Hyderabad: Central Institute of English and Foreign Language.

Arambam, L. 1991. Manipur as a Ritual Theater State. In N. Sanajaoba. (ed.). *Manipur Past and Present*. New Delhi: Mittal Publications.

Aruna Devi, Kh. 1990. *An Attitudinal Study of College Teachers (in Manipur) Towards English: An Empirical Study*. M. Phil. Dissertation. Imphal: Manipur University.

Bach, E. and Harnish, R.N. 1979. *Linguistic Communication and Speech Acts.* Cambridge, Mass: MIT Press.

Bailey, R. and Gorlach, M. 1982. *English as a World Language.* Ann Arbor: Michigan University Press.

Bambose, A. 1976. 'The changing role of the mother tongue in education.' In A. Bambose (edn). *Mother tongue in Education.* Paris: UNESCO PRESS

Bansal, R.K., A. 1976. *The Intelligibility of Indian English.* Monograph No. 4 Hyderabad: Central Institute of English and Foreign Languages. 2nd edn.

Barnes, Sir Edward. 1932. *The History of Royal College* (Colombo). Colombo Academy.

Barpujari, H.K. (ed.). 1992 *Comprehensive History of Assam.* 5 vols. Guwahati: Publication Board, Assam.

Barpujari H.K. and N. Sarma. 1993. *Reform and Regeneration.* In Barpujari (ed.). Vol. 5

Barpujari, H. K. 1996. *Assam in the Days of the Company.* Shillong: North-Eastern Hill University Publications.

Baruah, S.1999. *India Against Itself.* Delhi: Oxford University Press.

Bell, R.T. 1976. *Sociolinguistics: Goals, Approaches and Problems.* London: Batsford.

Bell, R.T. 1981. *An Introduction to Applied Linguistics: Approaches and Methods in Language Teaching* London: Batsford Academic and Educational.

Berns, M.S. 1985. *Functional Approaches and Communicative Competence: English Language Teaching in non-native contexts.* Ph.D. Dissertation. University of Illinois at Urban Champaign.

Bickerton, 1975. *Dynamics of a Creole System.* Cambridge: Cambridge University Press.

Bloomfeild, L.1935. *Language.* London: Allen and Unwin.

Bolinger, D.1973. Truth is a Linguistic question. *Language* 49:539-50.

Bolinger, D. 1980. *Language: The Loaded Weapon*. London: Longman.

Brass, P.R., 1974. *Language, Religion and Politics in North India*. Cambridge: Cambridge University Press

Britto, F.1986. *Diglossia: A Study of the Theory*. Washington DC: Georgetown University Press.

Brown, G. and Yule, G. 1983. Discourse Analysis, Cambridge: Cambridge University Press

Brown, H.D. 1980. *Principles of Language Learning and Teaching*. Engelwood Cliffs, N.J.: Prentice-Hall.

Brumfit, C.D. (ed.). 1982. *English for International Communication*. Oxford: Pergamon Institute of English.

Brumfit, C. J. 1984. *General English Syllabus Design: ELT Documents 118*. Oxford: Pergamon Press.

Census of India. 1981. *Manipur, Series-12, Part-I to V*. Delhi: Manager of Publications, 1985.

Census of India. 1991. Serise-1 India. Paper 2. of 1992. New Delhi: Registrar General and Census Çommissioner.

Census of India. 1991. *Series-15 Manipur of Paper-1 of 1991* Imphal: Director of Census Operations.

Chaddha, R. 1987. *A Cross-Cultural Interaction in the Novels of Kamala, Markandeya and Ruth Jhabvala. A Select Comparative Study*. Ph.D. Dissertation, Shimla: Himachal Pradesh University.

Chaklader, S. 1990. *Sociolinguistics (A Guide to Language Problems in India)*, New Delhi: Mittal Publications.

Chakravarti, R. 1986. *People of Manipur*. Delhi: B.R. Publications Corporation.

Chambers, J.K. and Trudgill, P. 1980. *Dialectology*. Cambridge: Cambridge University Press.

Chatterjee, P. 1986. *Nationalist Thought and the Colonial World: A Derivative Discourse.* London: Zed/Delhi: Oxford University Press.

Chatterjee, S.K. 1943. *Language and the Linguistic Problem*. London: Oxford University Press.

Chatterjee, S.K. 1960. *The Place of Assam in the History* and Civilization of India. Gauhati: Gauhati University.

Chatterjee, S.K. 1967. *Religion and Cultural Integration in India*. Imphal, (Publisher not mentioned).

Chatterjee, S.K., 1974. *Kirata-Jana-Kriti: The Indo-Mongoloids*. Calcutta: Asiatic Society of Bengal.

Cheshire, J. (ed.). 1991. *English Around the World*. Cambridge: Cambridge University Press.

Chomsky, N.1981, *Lectures on Government and Binding*. Dordrecht: Foris.

Chomsky, N.1986 *Knowledge of Language*. New York: Praeger.

Choudury, Sujit. 1999. *The North East: A Concept Reexamined*. In Aggarwal, K.S. (ed.). pp. 90-97

Coulmas, F. 1992. *Language and the Economy*. Oxford: Blackwell.

Cooper, R.L. (ed.). 1982. *Language Spread: Studies in Diffusion of Language Change*. Bloomington, IN: Indiana University Press.

Corder, S.P. 1974. *An Intermediate English Practice Book*. Madras: Longman.

Crewe, W. (ed.). 1977. *The English Language in Singapore*. Singapore: Eastern University Press.

Crystal, D.1985. How many millions? The Statistics of English Today. *English Today*, 1 January, 1985.

Crystal, D.1995. *The Cambridge Encyclopedia of the English Language*. Cambridge: Cambridge University Press.

Das, N.K. 1989. *Ethnic Identity, Ethnicity and Social Stratification in North-East India*. Delhi: Inter-India Publications.

Das, Parag Kumar. 1992. *Rastodrohir Dinlipi* (*Diary of an Enemy of The State*), Guwahati: Udangssri Prakaxon.

Das, R.K. 1985. *Manipur Tribal Scene*. New Delhi: Inter-India Publications.

Das, Susanta K. 1989. *Spotlight on Assam.* (Chandrapur), Maharastra: Premier Book Service.

Dasgupta, J. 1970. *Language Conflict and National Development: Group Politics and National Language Policy in India.* Bombay: Oxford University Press.

Dasgupta, P.1993. *The Otherness of English: India's Auntie Tongue Syndrome.* New Delhi: Sage.

Day, Richard R. 1985. *The ultimate inequality: linguistic genocide.* In Wolfson et at. (ed.). 1985, pp. 163-181

Dayananda, J.T. 1986. Plain English in the United States. *English Today,* Vol.5, 13-16.

Deen, E.W. 1886 *Gazetteer of Manipur.* Calcutta: Govt. Press.

Dissanayake, W. and Nichter, M.1987. Native sensibility and literary discourse. In Smith, L.E. (ed.). *Discourse Across Cultures: Strategies in World Englishes.* London: Prentice-Hall International.

Dissanayake, W. 1985. Towards a decolonized English: South Asian Creativity in Fiction. *World Englishes,* 4.2. pp. 233-242.

Dittmar, N. 1976. *A Critical Survey of Sociolinguistics: Theory and Applications.* New York: St. Martin's Press.

Dulay, H., Burt, M. and Krashen, S.1982. *Language Two.* New York: Oxford University Press.

Dustoor, P.E. 1968. *The World of Words Bombay*: Asia Publishing House.

Elwin, Verrier (ed.). 1969. *The Nagas in the Nineteenth Century.* Bombay: Oxford University Press.

Elwin, Verrier (ed.). 1961. *Nagaland,* Shillong: Research Department, Governor's Secretariat.

Fasold, R.W. 1972. *Tense Marking in Black English: A Linguistic and Social Analysis.* Washington, DC. : Centre for Applied Linguistics.

Firth , J. R. 1957.*Papers in Linguistics.* London: Oxford University Press.

Fishman, J.A. 1966. *Language Loyalty in the United States.* The Hague: Mouton.

Fishman, J.A., 1968. Sociolinguistic perspectives on the study of bilingualism. *Linguistics* 39: 21-4

Fishman, J.A. 1971. *Advances in the Sociology of Language.* The Hague: Mouton.

Fishman, J.A., 1972. *Sociolinguistics: A Brief Introduction.* Massachusetts: Newbury House Publishers, Inc.

Fishman, J.A., Cooper, R.L. and Conrad, A.W. (eds.). 1977. *The Spread of English: The Sociology of English as an Additional Language.* Rowley, MA: Newbury House.

Foster B.1968. *The Changing English Language.* London: Macmillan.

Foucault, M. 1980. *Power-Knowledge: Selected Interviews and Other Writings,* 1972-77. (ed.). C. Gordon; (Tr.) C. Gordon.

Gait, Edward A. 1990. [1905]. *A History of Assam.* Guwahati: Lawyer's Book Stall.

Gal, S. 1979. *Language Shift.* New York: Academic Press

Gandhi. R. 1984. *I am Thou: Meditations on the Truth of India.* Pune: Indian Philosophical Quarterly Publications.

Gangte, T.S. 1989. *Anglo-Kuki Relation since 1848 to 1937*. Imphal.

Gardner, R.C. 1985. *Socio Psychology and Second Language Learning: The Role of Attitudes and Motivation.* London: Edward Arnold.

Gardner, R.C. 1988. The socio-educational models of second language learning: assumptions, findings and issues. *Language Learning.* 38.1:101-26.

Gardner, R.C. and Lambert, W.E. 1972. *Attitudes and Motivation in Second Language Learning.* Rowley, Mass: Newbury House.

Gass, S. and Schachter, J. (eds.). 1989. *Linguistics Perspectives on Language Acquisition.* New York: Cambridge University Press.

Gass, S. and Selinker, L. (eds.). 1983. *Language Transfer in Language Learning.* Rowley, Mass: Newbury House.

Gimson, A.C. 1962. *An Introduction to the Pronunciation of English.* London: Edward Arnold.

Gleason, Jr. H.A. 1965. *Linguistics and English.* New York: Holt, Rinehart and Winston, Inc.

Gokak, V.K. 1984. *English in India: Its Present and Future.* New Delhi: Asia Publishing House.

Goswami, S.1997. *Language Politics in Assam*. Delhi: Ajanta Publications.

Government of Manipur. 1982. *Guide to the Records of the Manipur Political Agency (1886-1907 A.D.),* Vol.2. Imphal: Manipur State Archives.

Government of Manipur.1984. *Key Indicators of Socio-Economic Survey.* Imphal: Directorate of Economics and Statistics.

Gower, Sir Ernest 1958. *The Complete Plain Words.* London.

Grant, Charles. 1831-32. Observations on the state of society among the Asiatic subjects of Great Britain, particularly with respect to morals, and the means of improving it. In *General Appendix to Parliament Papers, 1831-32.* London.

Grierson, G.A. 1904. *The Linguistic Survey of India. Vol. III, Part-I.* Calcutta: Government Press.

Grosjean, F. 1982. *Life with Two Languages: An Introduction to Bilingualism.* Cambridge, MA: Harvard University Press.

Guha, Amalendu. 1977. *Planter Raj to Swaraj: Freedom Struggle and Electoral Politics in Assam, 1826-1947.* New Delhi: People's Publishing House.

Gumperz, J. 1964. Hindi-Punjabi Code Switching in Delhi. In *Proceedings of Ninth International Congress of Linguists.* London: Mounton.

Gumperz, J. 1982. Conversational Code-switching in Gumperz, J. (ed.). *Discourse Strategies.* Cambridge: Cambridge University Press. 59-99

Gumperz, J.J. (ed.). 1982. *Language and Social Identity* Cambridge: Cambridge University Press.

Gupta, R.S., Abbi, A. and Aggarwal, K.S. 1995. *Language and The State: Perspectives on the Eighth Schedule.* New Delhi: Creative Books.

Gupta, R.S. and Aggarwal, K.S. 1998. *Harmony and Conflict: Studies in Indian Sociolinguistics.* New Delhi: Creative Books

Halliday, M.A.K. 1973. *Explorations in the Functions of Language.* London: Edward Arnold.

Halliday, M.A.K. 1982. *Language as Social Semiotic: The Social Interpretation of Language and Meaning.* Baltimore: University of Bark Press.

Halliday, M.A.K. and Hasan, R. 1976. *Cohesion in English.* London: Longman.

Halliday, M.A.K., Mclntosh A. and Strevens, P.D. 1964. The Linguistic Sciences and Language Teaching. London: Longman.

Haugen, E. 1985. The Language of imperialism: unity of pluralism? In Wolfson et al. (eds.). *Language Inequality.* The Hague: Mouten.

Heller, (ed.). 1988. *Code-switching: Anthropological and Sociolinguistic Perspectives.* The Hague: Mouton.

Hock, H. H. 1986. *Principles of Historical Linguistics.* Berlin and New York: Mouton de Gruyter.

Hodson, T.C. 1908. *The Meitheis.* London: David Nutlt.

Hudson, T.C. 1911. *The Naga Tribes of Manipur.* London: MacMillan.

Horam, M. 1977. *Social and Cultural Life of Nagas.* Delhi: B.R. Publishing Corporation.

Hosali, P. 1997. *Nuances of English in India: What the Butlers Really Said.* Pune: Centre for Communication Studies.

Heonigswald, H.1996. *Language Change and Linguistic Reconstruction.* Chicago: University of Chicago Press.

Hodson, R.A. 1980. *Sociolinguistics.* Cambridge: Cambridge University Press.

Huebner, T., and Ferguson, C.A. (eds.). 1991. *Crosscurrents in Second Language Acquisition and Linguistic Theories.* Amsterdam: John Benjamins.

Hughes, A. and Trudgill, P. 1979. *English Accents and Dialects: An Introduction to Social and Regional Varieties of British English.* London: Arnold.

Illich, I.1983. Vernacular values and education. In Bain, B. (ed.). *The Sociogenesis of Language and Human Conduct.* New York: Plenum Press. 461-96

Jespersen, O. 1968. *Growth and Structure of the English Language.* New York: The Free Press.

Johnstone, J. 1896. *Manipur and The Naga Hills.* (Reprint) Delhi: Vivek Publishing House, 1971.

Joychandra, N. (ed.). 1988. *Freedom:Prajantantra Supplement.* Imphal, August 15.

Kabui, G. 1991. *History of Manipur, Vol-1.* New Delhi: National Publishing House.

Kachru, B.B. 1976. *Indian English: A Sociolinguistic Profile of a Transplanted Language.* Mimeo.

Kachru, B.B.1978. Code-mixing as a Communicative Strategy in India. In Alatis, J.E. (ed.). *International Dimensions of Bilingual Education. Monograph Series on Languages and Linguistics.* Washington DC: Georgetown University Press. pp. 193-207.

Kachru B.B. 1981. Socially realistic Linguistics: the Firthian Tradition. *International Journal of the Sociology of Language,* 31, 65-89.

Kachru, B.B. 1982. *The Other Tongue: English Across Cultures.* Urbana: University of Illinois Press.

Kachru, B.B. 1982, The bilingual's Linguistic repertoire. In Hartfort, A.V. et al. (eds.). *Issue in Bilingual Education: The Role of the Vernacular.* New York: Plenum. pp. 25-52

Kachru, B.B. 1983. *The Indianization of English: The English Language in India.* New Delhi: Oxford University Press.

Kachru, B.B. 1984. *The Alchemy of English: social and functional power of non-native varieties.* In Kramarae et al. (eds.).

Kachru, B.B. 1985. Standard codifications and sociolinguistic realism: the English language in the Outer Circle. In Quirk, R. and Widdowson, H. (eds.). *English in the World: Teaching and Learning the Language And Literatures.* London: Cambridge University Press.

Kachru, B.B. 1986. *The Alchemy of English: The Spread, Functions and models of Non-native Englishes.* Oxford: Pergamon Press.

Kachru, B.B. 1986 ESP and non native varieties of English: toward a shift in paradigm. *Studies in the Linguistic Sciences,* 16.1.

Kachru, B.B. 1986. The bilingual's creativity and contract literatures. *Studies in Linguistic Sciences.* 16.1.

Kachru, B.B. 1986. The Power and Politics of English. *World Englishes,* 5.2-3.

Kachru, B.B. and Smith. L. (eds.). 1986. *The Power of English: Cross-cultural Dimensions in Literature and Media. Special issue of World Englishes* 5:2-3.

Kachru B.B. 1988. The spread of English and sacred linguistic cows. In Lowenberg, P.H. (ed.). *Languages Spread and Language Policy: Issues, Implications and Case Studies.* Washington DC: Georgetown University Press, pp. 207-28

Kapoor, K. and Gupta, R.S. 1990. *English in India.* Delhi: Kalinga Publications.

Kar, R.K. and J.L. Sharma, 1990. *Ethnic Identity of Tea Labour: A Case Study in Assam.* In B. Pakem. (ed.).

Karna, M.N. 1999. *Ethnic Identity and Socio-Economic Processes in North-East India.* In Aggarwal, K.S. (ed.).

Kosambi, D.D. 1970. *The Culture and Civilization of Ancient India in historical Outline.* Delhi: Vikas.

Katre, S.M. 1958. *The Formation of Konkani.* Pune: Deccan College of Post-graduate Research Institute.

Kazi, A.A. 1987. *Ethnicity and Education in Nation Building: the Case of Pakistan.* New York: University Press of America.

Kellerman, E. and Shrewood – Smith, M. 1986. *Cross linguistic*

Influence in Second Language Acquisition. Oxford: Pergamon Press.

Kent, R.G. 1923. *Language and Philosophy*. Boston: Marshall Jones.

Khanna, A.L. 1983. *A study of Some Learner Variables in Learner English as a Second Language*. Ph.D. Thesis, University of Delhi.

Khelchandra, N.1969. *Ariba Manipuri Sahityagi Itihas*. Imphal: Manipur Sahitya Parishad.

Khelchandra, N. 1985. *Catalogue of Old Manipuri Manuscripts*. Imphal: Manipur Sahitya Parishad.

Khelchandra, N. and Ibungohal, N. (eds.). 1967. *Cheitharol Kumbhaba*. Imphal: Manipur Sahitya Parishad.

Khubchandani, L.M. 1963. *The Acculturation of Indian Sindhi to Hindi: A Study of Languages in Contact*. Ph. D. Dissertation, University of Pennsylvania,

Khubchandani, L.M. 1969. Functional importance in India a poddar, A (ed.). *Language and Society in India*. Shimla: Indian Institute of Advanced Study.

Khubchandani, L.M. 1972. Mother tongue in multilingual societies. In Chandra Shekhar, A. (ed.). *Economic and Socio-Cultural Dimensions of Regionalization*. New Delhi: Registrar General of India.

Khubchandani, L.M. 1974. Fluidity in mother tongue identity. In *Applied Sociolinguistics Vol. II*. Copenhagen AILA Proceedings. Heidelberg: J. Gross

Khubchandani, L.M. 1981. *Language Education, Social Justice, Serial: In search of Tomorrow*. Vol.2. Pune: Centre for Communication Studies.

Khubchandani, L.M. 1983. *Plural Languages, Plural Cultures: Communication, Identity and Sociopolitical Change in Contemporary India*. Honolulu: University of Hawaii Press.

Khubchandani, L.M. 1991. *Language Culture and Nation Building: Challenges of Mordenization*. Shimla: Indian Institute of Advanced Study.

Khubchandani, L.M. 1997. *Revisualizing Boundaries, a Plurilingual Ethos.* New Delhi: Sage.

Kiparsky, P. 1968. Linguistic Universals and Linguistic Change. In Boch, E. and Harms, R.T. (eds.). *Universals in Linguistic Theory.* New York: Holt, Rinehart and Winston.

Klein, W. 1986. *Second Language Acquisition.* Cambridge: Cambridge University Press.

Klima, E.S. 1964, Negation in English. In Fodor, J.A. and Katz, J.J. (ed.). *The Structure of Languages: Reading in the Philosophy of Language.* Engelwood Cliffs, N. J. : Prentice-Hall.

Kothari, D.S. 1966. *Report of the Education Commission, 1964-66: Education and National Development.* Publication No. 1198. New Delhi: Department of Education, Government of India.

Kramarae, C, M. Schulz and W.M. O'Barr. (eds.). 1984. *Language and Power.* Beverely Hills, CA: Sage Publications.

Krashen, S.1981. *Second Language Acquisition and Second Language Learning.* Oxford: Pergamon Press.

Krishnaswamy, N.1971. *An Introduction of Linguistics for Language Teaching.* Bombay: Somaiya Publications.

Kumar, B.B. 1994. *Higher Education in North-East India.* New Delhi: Omsons Publications.

Kuppuswamy, B.1962. *Manual of Socio-economic Status. Scale* (urban). Delhi: Manasayan.

Labov, W.1966. *The Social Stratification of English in New York City.* Washington DC: Centre for Applied Linguistics.

Labov, W. 1970. The Study of Language in its Social Context. *Studium Generale.* 23, 1, 32-87.

Lado, R.1957. *Linguistic Across Cultures.* Michigan: University of Michigan Press.

Lakoff, R. 1972. Language in context. *Language.* 48.907-27.

Lakoff, R. 1975, linguistic theory and real world. *Language Learning.* 25.2: 309-38.

Lal, P.1987. *The Alien Insiders.* Calcutta: Writers' Workshop.

Larsen-Freeman, D.1986. *Techniques and Principles in Language Teaching* New York: Oxford University Press.

Larsen-Freeman, D. and Long, M.1991. *An Introduction to Second Language Acquisition Research.* London: Longman

Le Page, R.B. and Tabourett-Keller, A.1985. *Acts of Identify: Creole-based Approaches to Language and Ethnicity.* Cambridge: Cambridge University Press.

Leibowitz, A.H. 1969. English Literacy: legal sanction for discrimination. *Notre Dame Lawyer.* Fall 5,7, pp. 7-67

Lele, J.K. and R. Singh. 1989. *Language and Society: Steps toward an Integrated Theory.* Leiden: Brill.

Littelwood, W.1961. *Communicating Language Teaching,* Cambridge: Cambridge University Press.

Llamzon, T.A. 1969. *Standard Filipino English.* Manila: Ateneo University Press.

Lokendrajit, S. 1986. Identity and Crisis of Identity: A case study of Manipur. *Proceedings of North East India History Association.* Shillong: NEHU 337-346.

Lowenberg, P. 1984. *English in the Malay Archipelago: Nativization and its functions in a Sociolinguistic Area.* Ph. D. Dissertation University of Illinois at Urbana – Champaign.

Lowenberg, P.H. 1986. Sociolinguistic context and second Language Acquisition: acculturation and creativity in Malayasian English. *World Englishes,* 5.1: 71-83.

Lowenberg, P.H. 1986. *Language Spread and Language Policy: Issues, Implications, and Case Studies.* GURT 1987. Washington DC: Georgetown University Press.

Lowenberg, P.H. and Sridhar, S. N. (eds.). 1986. World Englishes and Second Language Acquisition Research. *Special Issue of World Englishes, 5.1.*

Lukmani, Y. 1972, Motivation to learn and Language proficiency. *Language Learning.* 22:261-73.

Lyczak, R., Fu, and H.O.A. 1979. Attributes of Hong Kong bilinguals towards English and Chinese Speakers. *Journal of Cross Cultural Psychology* 74: 25-389.

Mackey, W.F. 1973 (1966). Applied Linguistics. In Allen,J.P.B. And Corder, SP (eds.). *Readings for Applied Linguistics: The Edinburgh Course in Applied Linguistics.* Vols-4. London: Oxford University Press.

Mandelbaum, D.G. 1970. *Society in India. Vol. – 2: Change and Continuity.* Berkeley: University of California Press

Mathur, C. 1991. *The Role of Attitudes and Motivation in Foreign Language Learning: the Case of German in India.* M.Phil Thesis, University of Delhi.

Mazrui, Ali. 1975. *The Political Sociology of the English Language.* The Hague: Mouton.

Mills, J.P. 1973 [1926]. *The Ao Nagas.* 2nd (ed.). Bombay: Oxford University Press.

Miltens, W.H. et al. 1970. *Attitudes to English Usage. An enquiry by the University of Newcastle upon Tyne.* Institute of New English Research Group. London: Oxford University Press.

Miri, M. 1982. *Linguistic Situation in North-East India.* Shillong: NEISSR

Misra, Udayan. 1988, *North-East India: Quest for Identity.* Guwahati: Omsons Publications.

Mohan, R. (ed.). 1978. *Indian Writing in English.* Delhi: Orient Longman.

Muhlhausler, P.1985. Patterns of contact, mixture, creation and activization. Their contribution to a general theory of language. In Bailey, C.J.N. and Harris, R. (eds.). *Developmental Mechanism of Language.* Oxford: Pergamon Press.

Mukherjee, A. 1980. *Language Maintenance and Language Shift among Punjabis and Bengalis in Delhi: A Sociolinguistic Perspective.* Ph.D. Thesis, University of Delhi, Delhi.

Nadkarni, M.V. 1978. Cultural Pluralism as a national resource. Strategies for language education: In Author, Y. (ed.). *Language*

Education in Multilingual Societies. Singapore: SEAMEO Regional Language Centre.

Nandy, A.1983. *The Intimate Enemy: Loss and Recovery of Self Under Colonialism.* Delhi: Oxford University Press.

Nemser, W. 1971. Approximative systems of foreign language learners. *International Review of Applied Linguistics* 9.2: 115-23.

Neog, M. 1976. *Annals of Assam Sahitya Sabha* [Axom Xahitya Xabha], 1917-75. Jorhat: Axon Xahitya Xabha

Neog, M. 1983. Atrocity in Assam. *New Republic.* March 21

Nichols, P.C. 1984. Networks and hierarchies: language and social stratification. In Kramarae et al. 1984, pp. 23-42

Nickel, G. 1975. Objective and subjective difficulties in connection with foreign language acquisition. In Telegdi, Z. et al. (eds.). *Modern Linguistics and Language Teaching. Proceedings of the International Conference at Budapest, 1-5 April 1971.* Budapest: Akadenial Kiado.

Nilabir, S. 1991. The Revivalist Movement of Sanamahism. In N.Sanajaoba (ed.). *Manipur past and Present.*

Noss, R.B. (ed.). 1983. *Varieties of English in South East Asia.* Anthology Series 11. Singapore: Singapore University Press.

Oller, J.Jr. and Conrad, C.A. 1971. The close procedures and ESL proficiency. *Language Learning* 21: 183-95.

Oppenheim, A.N. 1966. *A Questionnaire Design and Attitude Measurement.* London: Heinman.

Orwell, S. and I. Angus. 1968. *The Collected Essays, Journalism and Letters of George Orwell.* London: Secker and Warburg.

Paikeday, T.M. 1985. *The Native Speaker is Dead.* Toronto: Paikeday Publishing.

Pakem, B. (ed.). 1987. *Nationality, Ethnicity, and Cultural Identity in Northern East India.* New Delhi: Omsons Publications.

Pannicker, K.M. 1961. *Asia and Western Dominance: A Survey of the Vasco Da Gama Epoch on Asian History, 1498-1945.* London: George Allen & Judith.

Parasher, S.V. 1979. *Certain Aspects of the Functions and Form of Indian English: a Sociolinguistic Study.* Central Institute of English and Foreign Languages, Hyderabad. Unpublished Ph.D. Dissertation.

Parasher, S.V.1980. Mother Tongue English diglossia: a case study of Indian bilinguals language use. *Anthropological Linguistics* 22.4: 151-68.

Parasher, S.V. 1991. *Indian English: Functions and Form.* New Delhi: Bahri Publications.

Pattanayak, D.P 1981. *Multilingualism and Mother Tongue Education.* Delhi: Oxford University Press.

Patter, S. 1975. *Changing English.* London: Deutsch, 2nd revised edition.

Pemberton, R.B. 1835. *Report of Eastern Frontier of British India.* Gauhati: Department of Historical and Antiquarian Studies.

Phillipson. R. 1992. *Linguistic Imperialism.* Oxford: Oxford University Press.

Philipson, R. 1994. *Linguistic Human Rights: Overcoming Linguistic Discrimination.* Berlin: Mouton de Gruyter.

Phukan, U. 1984. *The Ex-Tea Garden Labour Population in Assam.* Delhi: D.R. Publishing House.

Platt, J. and Weber, H. 1980. *English in Singapore and Malaysia: Facts, Features, Functions.* Kuala Lumpur: Oxford University Press.

Platt. J. and Weber, H. and Ho, M.L. 1984. *The New Englishes.* London: Routedge & Kegen Paul.

Politzer, R.L. 1965. *Foreign Language Learning: A Linguistic Introduction.* New Jersey: Prentice-Hall.

Prabhu, N.S. 1980. *Communicational Teaching Project*. Bangalore: Regional Institute of English. 22, 64.

Prabhu, N.S. 1987. *Second Language Pedagogy.* Oxford: Oxford University Press.

Pride, J.B. 1979. A traditional view of speech functions and

codes-witching. In McCormack, M.C. and S.A. Worm (eds.). *Language and Society: Anthropological Issues*. The Hague: Mouton.

Promodini, N. 1989. *A Social Grammar of Meiteilon*. Unpublished Ph.D. Dissertation, University of Manipur.

Quirk, R., Greenbaum, S., Leech, G., and Svartvik, J. 1972. *A Grammar of Contemporary English*. London: Longman.

Quirk, R. 1985. The English language in a global context. In Quirk, R. and Widdowson, H. (eds.). *English in the World: Teaching and Learning the Language and Literatures*. London: Cambridge University Press..

Quirk, R. and Widdowson, H. (eds.). 1985. *English in the World: Teaching and Learning the Language and Literatures*. London: Cambridge University Press.

Radhakrishnan, S. 1949. *The Report of the University Education Commission, 1948-49*. New Delhi: Department of Education, Government of India.

Raine, K. and Sethna, K.D. 1986. *The English Language and the Indian Spirit: Correspondence between Raine and Sethna*. Pondichery: Sri Aurobindo Ashram.

Ramaih, L.S. 1985. *Communicative Language Teaching: A Bibliography*. Gurgoan, Haryana: Indian Documentation Service.

Ramani, E. 1987. Theorizing from the classroom. *ELT Journal 41*. 1:3-11

Rao, G.1954. *Indian Words in English: A study in Indo – British Cultural and Linguistic Relations*. Oxford: Oxford University Press.

Ray, J. 1973. *History of Manipur*. 2nd Edition. Calcutta: East Light Book House.

Richards, J., Platt, J. and Weber, H. 1985. *Longman Dictionary of Applied Linguistics*. Essex. London.

Robinett, B.W. and Schachter, J. (eds.). 1983. *Second Language Learning: Contrastive Analysis, Error Analysis and Related Aspects*. Ann Arbor, MI: University of Michigan Press.

Robinson, W.P. 1971. Social factor and language development in Primary School Children. In Huxley, R. and Ingram, E. (eds.). *Language Asquisition. Models and Methods.* New York: Academic Press.

Rose, L.E. 1994. *The Nepali Ethnic Community in the Northeast of the Subcontinent. Ethnic Studies Report.* 12,1 (January).

Russel, R. 1938. *Power.* London: Unwin Books.

Rutherford, W.D. (ed.). 1984. *Language Universals and Second Language Acquisition.* Amsterdam: John Benjamins.

Sadock, J.M. 1974. *Toward a Linguistic Theory of Speech Acts*. New York: Academic Press.

Sahgal, A. 1983. *A Sociolinguistic Study of the English Spoken by Delhi Elite.* Unpublished M. Phil., Thesis. University of Delhi.

Sanajaoba, N. (ed.). 1991. *Manipur Past and Present Vol.2.* Delhi: Mittal Publications.

Sarmah, N.1965 *Meeteilon.* Imphal. Students Book Store.

Saville-Troike, M.1984. What really matters in second language learning for academic achievements? *TESOL Quarterly 18:* 199-219

Schucrardt, H. 1981. Indo English in Gilbert, G. C. et al. *Pidgin and Creole Languages: Selected Essays by Schuchard (1981).* London: Cambridge University Press

Selinker, L.1972. Interlanguage. IRAL 10.3:219-31

Sey, K.A. 1973. *Ghanaian English: An Exploratary Survey.* London and Basingstoke: Macmillan.

Shackle, C.1987. Speakers of Indian Language. In Swan, M. and Smith, Bernard (eds.). *Learner English: A Teachers Guide to Interference and Other Problems.* Cambridge University Press.

Shah, A.B. 1968 (ed.). *The Great Debate.* Bombay: Lalvani Publishing House.

Shakespear, J. 1912 *Lushai-Kuki Clan.* London.

Shils, E. 1974. The academic professions in India. In A. Singh and P.G. Altbach. (eds.). *The Higher Learning in India.* Bombay: Vikas Publishing House.

Sidhu, C.D. 1976. *An Intensive Course in English.* New Delhi: Orient Longman.

Sinclair, J. 1986. An approach to the teaching of English language at University level. In *Rajasthan University Studies in English.* Vol. XVIII. Jaipur.

Singh, J.N. 1992. *Social Movements in Manipur.* New Delhi: Mittal Publications.

Singh, K.B. (ed.). 1976. *An Introduction to Tribal Language and Culture of Manipur.* (7 tribes). Imphal: Manipur State Kala Akademi.

Singh, Kh. Chandrasekhar. (ed.). 1975. *Loiyumba Shinyen.* Imphal: Manipur Sahitya Parishad.

Singh, M. Chandra, 1979. *Poireiton Khunthok.* Imphal: Manipur Sahitya Parishad.

Singh, O.K. 1978. *A Live Megalithic Culture in Manipur. Recent Advances in Indo-Pacific Pre-History.* Poona.

Singh, Y.K. 1971. *Poireiton Khunthokpa.* Imphal: Manipur Sahitya Parishad

Singh, Y.W. 1966. *An Early History of Manipur.* Imphal: Students' Book Store.

Smith, L.E. (ed.). 1981. *English for Cross-cultural Communication.* London: Macmillan.

Smith, L.E. (ed.). 1983. *Readings in English as an International Language.* Oxford: Pargamon Press.

Smith, Anne-Marie. 1986. *Papua New Guinea English.* Ph.D. Dissertation, The University of Papua New Guinea.

Smith, L.E. (ed.). 1987. *Discourse Across Cultures: Strategies in World Englishes.* London: Prentice-Hall International.

Sridhar, K.K. 1989. *English in Indian Bilingualism.* New Delhi: Manohar.

Sridhar, S.N. 1990. What are applied linguistics? *Studies in Linguistic Sciences.* 20.2: 165-76

Srivastava, R.N. 1977. Indian Multilingualism: myth and reality. In Shrama, P.G. and Kumar, S. (eds.). *Indian Bilingualism.* Agra: Kendriya Hindi Sansthan.

Steiner, G. 1975. *Why English?* Presidential address in 1975. London: The English Association.

Stockwell, R.P. and Macaulay, R.K.S. 1989. *Linguistics Change and Generative Theory.* Bloomington: Indiana University Press.

Strevens, P.1981. *Teaching English as an International Language.* Oxford: Pergamon Press.

Syngle, B.D. 1969. *A Description of Bengali English.* M.Litt. Dissertation, University of Delhi.

Szepe, G. 1975. Linguistics-applied linguistics-foreign language acquisition in Telegdi, Z. et al. (eds.).

Telegdi, Z. et al. (ed.). 1975. *Modern Linguistics and Language Teaching. Proceedings of the International Conference at Budapest.* 1-5 April 1971. Budapest: Akadeniai Kiado

The Orunodoi, 1846-1857. Guwahati: Assam Prakashan Parishad.

Thomason, S.G. and Koffman, T. 1988. *Language Contact and Creolization.* Berkelay: California University Press.

Tongue, R.K. 1974. *The English of Singapore and Malaysia.* Singapore: Eastern University Press.

Trivedi, H. and Mukherjee, M. (ed.). 1996. *Interrogating Post-Colonialism: Theory, Text and Context.* Shimla: Indian Institute of Advanced Study.

Trudgill, P. 1974. *The Social Differentiation of English in Norwich.* London: Cambridge University Press.

Trudgill P. (ed.). 1978. *Sociolinguistic Patterns in British English.* London: Arnold.

Trudgill, P. (ed.). 1984. *Applied Sociolinguistics.* New York: Academic Press.

Trudgill, P. and Hannah, J. 1982. *International English: A Guide to Varieties of Standard English.* London: Arnold.

UNESCO. 1953. *The Use of Vernacular Languages in Education.* Monograph on Fundamental Education. No. 8. Paris.

Vaiphei, P. S. 1986. *Church Growth Among the Hill Tribes in Manipur, North East India.* 2nd Edition. Imphal: Mrs. H. Vaiphei.

Velayudhan, S. (ed.). 1988. *Teaching English: Classroom Issues.* Bangalore: Macmillan.

Verma, S.K. 1974. *Introduction to English Language Teaching. Vol. I Linguistics.* Delhi: Oxford University Press.

Verma, S.K. 1980. Swadeshi English: form and function. *Indian Linguistics. 41,73-84.*

Verma, S.K. 1981. Politeness in Indian English ; an exploration in the functions of language? Paper presented at the Seminar on *Politeness Hierarchy in Indian Languages,* Hyderabad.

Verma, S.K. 1986. Language in Education in a Multilingual Society. Presidential Address delivered at the All India Conference of the Linguists.

Viswanathan, G.1990. *Masks of Conquest: Literary Study and British Rule in India.* Columbia: Columbia University Press.

Weiner, Myron, 1978. *Sons of the soil: Migration and Ethnic Conflict in India.* Princeton, N.J.: Princeton University Press.

Weinreich, U. 1953 (1963). *Languages in Contact: Findings and Problems.* The Hague: Mouton.

Widdowson, H.G. 1982. English as an International Language in Brumfit, C.J. (ed.). *English for International Communication* Oxford: Pergamon Press.

Widdowson, H.G. 1983. *Learning Purpose and Language Use.* Oxford: Oxford University Press.

Widdowson, H.G. 1984. *Exploitations in Applied Linguistics. Vol.2* Oxford: Oxford University Press

Wilkins, D.As. 1976. *Notional Syllabus.* Oxford: Oxford University Press.

Wolfram, N. and Judd, E. 1983. *Sociolinguistics and Language Acquisition.* Rowley, M.A.: Newbury House.

Wolfram, W. and Fasold, R.W. 1974. *The Study of Social Dialects in American English.* New Jersey: Prentice – Hall Inc.

Wong, M.J. 1982. *The Role of Attitudes and Motivation in Second Language Acquisition Among Adolescent Native Chinese Speakers in the US.* Ph. D. Thesis, University of San Francisco, California.

Zentella, A.C. 1981. Language variety among Puerto Ricans. In Ferguson, C.A. et al. (eds.). Language in the U.S.A. Cambridge: Cambridge University Press.

INDEX